Letters

for every
occasion

Basildon Bond Letters for every occasion

Edited by Derek Hall

W. Foulsham & Co. Ltd.
London · New York · Toronto · Cape Town · Sydney

W. Foulsham & Company Limited
Yeovil Road, Slough, Berkshire, SL1 4JH

ISBN 0-572-01213-6

The publishers would like to point out that all the names of people,
companies, publications, trade goods, etc., as well as all the addresses to be
found in this book, are intended to be entirely fictional. Any similarities with
actual names are entirely coincidental.

Photoset and printed in Great Britain by David John Services Limited,
Maidenhead, Berkshire, and St Edmundsbury Press, Bury St Edmunds,
Suffolk.

CONTENTS

INTRODUCTION

Someone once said: 'The letter you write is you.' In many ways this is — and should be — true, and it is therefore very important that every letter you send should be your best work so that its recipient will gain a good impression of you.

The letters in this book are designed to cover all sorts of situations in personal, official (a letter to a government body or bank, for example) and business life. However, it is unlikely that you will find exactly what you are looking for in every case. The letters here should be used as examples, providing a framework and setting the correct tone for your own expression.

Content

What you say and how you say it is just as important in a personal letter as it is in an official or business letter, and a number of general points apply equally to each.

1 Clarity of thought: if you do not organise your own thoughts clearly before writing a letter, it will inevitably appear rambling and confused to the recipient. So decide what you want to say before you write. If you have a number of points to make, jot them down and arrange them in a logical order. You will probably find that some are repetitive or are not relevant. Cut them out ruthlessly. Then get straight to the point — and stick to it!

2 Clarity of expression: having decided what you want to say, you must also make sure that the recipient will understand it. Try to use short words and short sentences which convey the message simply and clearly. Long words and complex grammatical constructions are more difficult to read and are often imprecise. If you do sometimes use long words — and they cannot always be avoided — get into the habit of checking them in a dictionary. It is surprising how often they do not convey quite the meaning you intended. Checking them in a dictionary will also ensure they are correctly spelt.

Similarly, try not to use too much technical jargon. You want the recipient to understand the letter, not marvel at your knowledge — which may be quite meaningless to him.

3 Clichés: avoid using 'commercial' letter phrases such as 'Permit me to state' or 'We beg to acknowledge receipt of your letter'. These are clichés and may add little or nothing to your meaning. The first example could be dispensed with altogether — just go ahead and state; the second would be better written, 'Thank you for your letter'. Other examples are:

'We take pleasure in advising' (write: 'We are pleased to let you know').
'Your goodself' (write: 'You').
'Your letter has come to hand' (write: 'Your letter has arrived').

'I await the pleasure of a reply' (write: 'I look forward to hearing from you' — or leave out).

4 Courtesy and honesty: these qualities are important in a letter not merely because they are the correct way to behave, but also because you are committing yourself to paper. If you write anything libellous, for example, you may well end up in court. Remember, it is not only the person you are writing to who may read the letter.

If you are writing a letter of complaint, think very carefully before choosing your words. Try not to be abusive, but if you simply must get it off your chest, then write it and sleep on it. After that you will probably prefer to throw it away rather than send it.

5 Check the letter: always date the letter and check that the recipient's name, initials and address are given correctly. Read the letter over before sealing it. Check any facts and figures and, if enclosures are mentioned, make sure that they really are enclosed. Finally, make certain that you put the letter in the right envelope.

Writing materials

The notepaper should be good quality, and plain, with no lines, coloured borders or pictures. Sheets of A4 size are handy to read and preferable to either folded notepaper or notelets for everything but personal or intimate correspondence. Larger, foolscap sheets are suitable for longer business letters. The paper and the envelope should match, except in special situations such as when several sheets are enclosed in one large envelope.

If you are writing the letter by hand, black or blue inks are usually the most satisfactory colours.

Layout and presentation

A badly laid out letter where the typing is ragged, or the writing straggling and slanted, for example, immediately creates a bad impression. It suggests an offhand approach and encourages the same response in the reader. A well presented letter, especially a business or official letter, does just the opposite. If you have taken some care with the production, you are paying the reader a compliment and he or she is more likely to take you and the letter seriously.

If you are writing a business letter, it should be typed. In other cases, handwriting — as long as it is legible — is perfectly acceptable and is indeed preferable when the letter is of a personal nature.

Most letters can be divided into: sender's address, date, recipient's address, opening greeting, main text, complimentary close and signature. Some letters may also include a heading, and space may be left for references, both sender's and recipient's. The basic layout of these parts is as follows.

1 Sender's address: if you are not using headed notepaper this should go in the top right corner of the sheet. Each line may be indented (the address is 'stepped') or not.

2 Date: leave a space and put the date below the sender's address, in line with the first line of the address.

7

3   Recipient's address: leave a space (at least a line space if typing) after the date and write the address on the left side of the sheet. It is not normally stepped. In a personal letter, you may omit this.

4   Opening greeting: leave a space after the recipient's address and begin 'Dear Sir', or whatever is appropriate, directly below.

5   **Main text: leave a space before beginning the main body of the letter. Paragraphs may be indented or not (see below). Leave a space between paragraphs.**

6   Complimentary close: leave a space between the final paragraph and the complimentary close, which may be written on the left side of the sheet, or towards the right.

7   Signature: the signature comes directly below the complimentary close. Even if the signature is legible, it is helpful to print or type the writer's name underneath and, if appropriate, his or her job title or position.

8   References: these are normally written on separate lines, beginning opposite the first line of the recipient's address and directly below the date, leaving a space.

9   Heading: it is sometimes helpful to include an underlined heading, such as Mortgage policy no 2345. It is placed after the opening greeting, and before the first paragraph, leaving a space above and below. It may be written on the left side of the sheet, or centred.

Indented or blocked style?

The choice of indenting the sender's address and paragraphs in the main text, and the alternative positions of the heading and the complimentary close, represent two different styles within the basic layout. Either is correct, but it is important not to mix the styles.

The *blocked style* contains no indentations, and the heading and complimentary close are written on the left side of the sheet. The alternative, called the *indented style,* is more appropriate if you are writing a letter by hand.

Whatever style you use, leave an adequate space after closing the letter for your signature. For personal letters, just sign your name. For business letters, write or type your name, and position if relevant, beneath your signature.

Example 1   Blocked style

Double Dealers,
12 Fairview Lane,
Marshgate,
Surrey,
BX7 2JG

7th October 19 -

Mrs J. R. Noakes,   Our ref. PL 27B
14 Better Road,
Tinton,   Your ref.
Devon,
SB9 6PT

Dear Mrs Noakes,

Repairs to new garage doors

I am sorry that you are not satisfied with the installation of new
garage doors that was carried out on 22nd September. However, I
cannot agree to carry out the repairs you ask for without charging
a further fee.

It is unfortunate that you accidently reversed into the doors, but I
am not surprised that the hinges and bolts broke as a result. I
think in this case it would be fair to blame the car and not poor
workmanship on our part.

However, since the repairs needed are fairly minor, I am prepared
to refit the doors and charge only for the cost of the new hinges
and bolts.

I hope this will be satisfactory.

Yours sincerely,

Norman Aldwin

Norman Aldwin
Managing Director

Example 2   Indented style

Double Dealers,
12 Fairview Lane,
Marshgate,
Surrey,
BX7 2JG

7th October 19 -

Mrs J. R. Noakes,
14 Better Road,
Tinton,
Devon,
SB9 6PT

Our ref. PL 27B

Your ref.

Dear Mrs Noakes,

<u>Repairs to new garage doors</u>

I am sorry that you are not satisfied with the installation of new garage doors that was carried out on 22nd September. However, I cannot agree to carry out the repairs you ask for without charging a further fee.

It is unfortunate that you accidently reversed into the doors, but I am not surprised that the hinges and bolts broke as a result. I think in this case it would be fair to blame the car and not poor workmanship on our part.

However, since the repairs needed are fairly minor, I am prepared to refit the doors and charge only for the cost of the new hinges and bolts.

I hope this will be satisfactory.

Yours sincerely,

Norman Aldwin
Managing Director

Punctuation style in letters

Two methods of punctuation are commonly used when writing letters, excluding the main text where the normal rules of punctuation apply.

The first method, most suitable when writing by hand, is shown in the previous examples. Each line of the address except the last is followed by a comma, as is the opening greeting and the complimentary close. There is no full stop after the post code, nor after the date, nor after the name or job title of the writer. Abbreviations, such as Rd (Road) Mr (Mister) ref. (reference) and Esq. (Esquire), take a full stop when the last letter of the abbreviation differs from the last letter of the abbreviated word. (In other words only when the work is a true abbreviation, and not a contraction.) Thus Esq. and ref. take a full stop, while Rd and Mr do not. The same applies to the initials before a person's name, which take a full stop.

The second method is simply to omit punctuation from all parts of the letter excluding the main text. This is known as the open punctuated style and is most often used together with the blocked style of layout.

How to begin a letter

1   Dear Sir,
2   Dear Madam,
    Either of the above is usual in all business correspondence.
3   Sir,
4   Madam,
    These are still sometimes used, but are more formal than 'Dear Sir' or 'Dear Madam'.
5   Dear Sirs,
    This is the correct opening when the letter is addressed to 'Messrs So and So'. As an alternative, 'Sirs', can be used if greater formality is required.
6   Gentlemen,
    Sometimes still used instead of (5) when you wish to be very formal or oratorical.
    Note that a letter begun in any of the above ways does not make clear to whom it is addressed. It is therefore imperative that if you are in fact writing to a particular person, their name and/or title should appear in the address.
7   Dear Mr Jones,
8   Dear Mrs Brown,
9   Dear Miss Smith,
10 Dear Ms Taylor,
    All the above are correct when the writer is personally acquainted with the person receiving the letter or has had previous correspondence with them. Ms is, however, best avoided if the lady's marital status can possibly be established.
11 Dear John Brown, or Dear Mary Smith,
    These are now quite acceptable, but are rather less formal than the earlier forms of address.
12 Dear Tom, or My Dear Tom,
    These are used between good friends, in either personal or business letters.

11

13 My Darling Tom, or My Dearest Mary,

These are correct for special cases of affection and should never be used in a business context.

How to close a letter

1 Yours faithfully,

A safe ending for most business letters when the formal 'Dear Sir' or 'Dear Madam' has been used at the beginning.

2 Yours sincerely, and Yours very sincerely,

Correct for more friendly business letters, written to someone addressed by name, such as 'Dear Mr Smith'.

3 Yours sincerely, or Best wishes,

A safe ending for all personal letters and business letters where the correspondents are well known to one another.

4 Yours affectionately,

Suitable for relations, would-be relations and between girlfriends, but now usually replaced by (3).

5 Faithfully yours, and (2) to (4)

The words can be reversed, though the result is slightly pompous.

6 Yours respectfully,

Used in a long letter that is in the form of a report. In other cases it should be used rarely, since it can seem servile.

7 Your obedient servant,

Only used in certain official letters.

8 Yours ever, or Love,

Only used when writing to a close friend.

Phrases for beginning letters

If you are looking for a phrase to start your letter, one of the following will probably suit your purpose:

I am very grateful for -
In reply to your letter of -
It was kind of you to -
I am sorry to tell you -
It is so long since you wrote -
I am wondering if you could -
As requested -
Thank you for -
I enclose -
Please -
Thank you for your letter of -
I am sorry to inform you that -
I greatly appreciate your -
With reference to your letter of -
Referring to your letter of -
I am anxious to hear from you concerning -
You may be interested to hear -
We wish to remind you that -

I have to point out -
Your letter gave me -
I have carefully considered your -
I would like to know -
I am writing to -
We recently wrote to you about -
Many thanks for the beautiful -
I know you will be sorry to hear that -
I am delighted to tell you that -

The address on the notepaper

1   The address of the sender may be ranged left or stepped; that of the recipient, if included, should be ranged left to the margin.
2   If you are writing to a particular person, put his or her name or title on the first line of the address. Depending on the degree of formality, you can write: 'T A Brown Esq.', 'Mr T A Brown', or 'Mr Tom Brown'. if you do not know the person's initials, write 'Mr Brown', not 'Brown Esq.'.

An alternative is to put <u>For the attention of Mr T A Brown</u> two lines above the address.
3   Do not write the name of a house in inverted commas. Thus, write Willow Farm, not 'Willow Farm'.
4   It used to be correct to follow the number of a house by a comma, but most people omit it nowadays.
5   The words 'Road', 'Street', 'Avenue', etc., should be written with a capital initial letter.
6   The words 'Road', 'Street', etc., may be shortened, if necessary, to 'Rd', 'St', etc.
7   Write the name of the town with capitals throughout, or just with a capitalised initial letter, followed on the next line by the name of the county, with the exception of large cities such as Liverpool or Manchester and county towns when the county name is unnecessary. Counties which can be abbreviated, such as Nottinghamshire (Notts), may be written in either style.
8   The post code should be placed after the name of the county (or county town) on its own on the final line.

Addressing an envelope

The address on an envelope gives the recipient his or her first impression of you. If it is well laid out, the impression will be a good one, but if the wording is badly arranged, it will certainly be unfavourable — if, that is, the letter arrives!

To space the wording properly, imagine a horizontal line cutting the envelope into two equal parts, one above the other. Start the person's name and address slightly below this imaginary line, towards the middle of the envelope.

Having written the name of the recipient, write the address in three, four or more lines, exactly as it appears in the letter. Each line should be either flush with the line above, or indented a little more than the one above, depending on the style adopted. Type or write the name of the town in capital letters, followed by the county name and post code on separate lines.

The Post Office requests writers to observe particularly the following rules for addressing envelopes correctly:

1   Use the number of the house, if it has one, and not just the name of the house.

2   In the case of flats, chambers and suites of offices give the number of the flat, etc.

3   Write the name of the street, road, etc. but only add a district within a town if there is more than one street of the same name in that particular town.

4   In country districts, the name of the hamlet or village is essential.

5   State the post town, that is, the centre to which the mail is sent.

6   Write the name of the county, except in the case of large towns or cities, such as London or Bristol, and those which give their names to counties, such as Gloucester.

7   Do not use the name of the county town, when the name of the county is intended. Thus do not write 'Cambridge' when 'Cambridgeshire' is correct.

Here are some examples:

1   Mr B A Williams
Willows
34 High Road
BROUGHTON
Sussex
BR5 4TR

2   John Davison Esq
Flat 2
38 Victoria Road
WESTBURY
Surrey
W17 9UG

Esq. and Mr are alternative forms for addressing gentlemen and it is wrong to use them together. If your letter begins 'Dear Sir', then the more formal method of address, using Esq., will be more suitable.

3   Mrs Paul Turnbell
51 Cadogan Avenue
WELLFORD
Lancashire
LA8 2FE

4   Mrs Jane Phillip
54 Wharf Rd
West Bridgford
SOTTON (Post town)
Surrey
SE9 4TR

A married woman is sometimes addressed by her husband's name or initials rather than her own, as in (3). However, most women now prefer to be addressed by their own first name.

5   Sir John Smith
    Cherry Hinton
    4 Garden Lane
    Bookham
    MAIDENHEAD (Post town)
    Berkshire
    MO6 2YF
6   Ms J Thompson
    14 Dean Lane
    ELY
    Cambridgeshire
    CF10 8YS

Ms may be used if you do not know whether the woman to whom you are writing is single or married. If you are writing to a married woman who prefers to use her maiden name, then you should address her as Ms or Miss, followed by her own Christian name or initials.

7   Mr Paul Stanley
    85 South Street
    LONDON
    NW1 7YG
8   For the attention of Mr B K Bugley
    Messrs J Ridley and Samuel
    2 High St
    READING
    Berkshire
    RE2 3JB

Messrs may be used when writing to a partnership, when the partners' names are given as part of the firm's name. If the envelope is marked For the attention of . . . use this method address in the letter. The opening should still be 'Dear Sirs', since the letter is addressed to the company.

The date

Every letter should be dated. There are many ways in which the date can be written. Forms (2) and (3) are the most generally accepted.

1 January 1 19—
2 January 1st 19—
3 1st January 19—
4 Jan 1 19—
5 1 January 19—
6 1 Jan 19—

The use of postcards

Blank (not 'holiday') postcards are a handy, quick and inexpensive way of sending messages, but they should not be over used. They may be used to send a hurried note of an impersonal nature, such as an acknowledgement, but there should be nothing private or intimate written on them. If the message is too personal, it is in bad taste. The sender may not mind how much of his news is broadcast, but the recipient may object.

It is not necessary to repeat the recipient's address in the main body of the text, nor to include the opening greeting (Dear Mr Brown etc.) or complimentary close.

Writing to persons of title

Special rules apply when writing to persons of title. In the list below, each example gives the correct wording of the title (used in the address) and the conventional opening and closing phrases.

THE QUEEN
Address: Her Majesty the Queen
Begin: Madam
            With my humble duty
End: I have the honour to remain (or to be)
            Madam
            Your Majesty's most humble and obedient servant

ROYAL PRINCES
Address: His Royal Highness
            The Prince of —
Begin: Sir
End: I have the honour to remain (or to be)
            Sir
            Your Royal Highness's most humble and obedient servant

ROYAL PRINCESSES
Address: Her Royal Highness
            The Princess of —
Begin: Madam
End: I have the honour to remain (or to be)
            Madam
            Your Royal Highness's most humble and obedient servant

DUKE
Address: His Grace the Duke of —
Begin: My Lord Duke
End: Yours faithfully

DUCHESS
Address: Her Grace the Duchess of —
Begin: Dear Madam
End: Yours faithfully

MARQUESS, EARL, VISCOUNT, BARON (Peers, other than a Duke)
Address: The Most Hon the Marquess of —
            The Rt Hon the Earl of —
            The Rt Hon the Viscount —
            The Rt Hon the Lord —
Begin: My Lord
End: Yours faithfully

WIFE OF A PEER, OTHER THAN A DUKE

The wife of a Marquess is a MARCHIONESS
The wife of an Earl is a COUNTESS
The wife of a Viscount is a VISCOUNTESS
The wife of a Baron is a BARONESS

Address: The Most Hon the Marchioness of —
           The Rt Hon the Countess of —
           The Rt Hon the Viscountess —
           The Rt Hon the Lady —
Begin: Dear Madam
End: Yours faithfully

BARONET
Address: Sir (Christian and Surname) Bt
Begin: Dear Sir
End: Yours faithfully

BARONET'S WIFE
Address: Lady (Surname only)
Begin: Dear Madam
End: Yours faithfully

KNIGHT
Address: Sir (Christian and Surname) with the appropriate letters after
           his name
Begin: Dear Sir
End: Yours faithfully

KNIGHT'S WIFE
Address: Lady (Surname only)
Begin: Dear Madam
End: Yours faithfully

ARCHBISHOP
Address: The Most Reverend the Lord Archbishop of —
Begin: Dear Archbishop
End: Yours sincerely

BISHOP
Address: The Right Reverend the Lord Bishop of —
Begin: Dear Bishop
End: Yours sincerely

DEAN
Address: The Very Reverend the Dean of —
Begin: Dear Dean
End: Yours sincerely

ARCHDEACON
Address: The Venerable the Archdeacon of —
Begin: Dear Archdeacon
End: Yours sincerely

AMBASSADOR
Address: His Excellency (followed by any style, title or rank, and name)
Begin: Sir
End: I have the honour to be
Sir
Your Excellency's obedient servant

GOVERNOR-GENERAL or GOVERNOR
Address: His Excellency
Name
Governor-General of —
or
Governor of —
Begin: Sir
or
My Lord (if a peer)
End I have the honour to be
Sir (My Lord, if a peer)
Your Excellency's obedient servant

MEMBER OF HER MAJESTY'S GOVERNMENT
Address: A letter sent to a Minister as the head of his department is addressed by his appointment only.
Begin: Dear Sir
End: Yours faithfully
   If the writer knows the Minister concerned, it is permissible to write to him by his appointment, for example:
Begin: Dear Prime Minister
Dear Lord Privy Seal
Dear Chancellor
End: Yours sincerely

LORD MAYOR
Address: The Right Honourable the Lord Mayor of —
Begin: My Lord Mayor
End: Yours faithfully

MAYOR OF A CITY
Address: The Right Worshipful the Mayor of —
Begin: Mr Mayor
End: Yours faithfully

ALDERMAN

Address: Alderman (followed by any title or rank, and name)
Begin: My Lord, Dear Sir, Dear Madam, or Dear Mr Alderman
End: Yours faithfully

COUNCILLOR

As for Alderman, substituting 'Councillor' for 'Alderman'.

MEMBER OF PARLIAMENT

As in private life, with the addition of the letters MP after the name.

INVITATIONS AND REPLIES

The most important point to remember when drafting an invitation, either written or printed, is to give details of the time, place and type of event — and your own name. It is surprising how many invitation cards have to be reprinted because one or other of these details have been omitted.

Information can also be conveyed through the style of the invitation; a formal invitation suggests a formal event, and so on. Choose the style to suit the occasion. If you are issuing printed invitations but feel they are too formal for some very close friends, a brief handwritten note in one corner will make the invitation much more personal.

If you receive an invitation, remember to reply to say whether you will or will not be attending. It is usual to reply in the same style as the invitation.

In this chapter, all sorts of invitations and replies are given as examples. Often, informal events are best arranged in person or by telephone but if you are planning something more elaborate or just wish to pay someone the courtesy of a written invitation you should find the appropriate wording.

Invitation to a wedding (formal)

Mr and Mrs John Fowler

request the pleasure of
the company of

(write the name of the guest(s))
at the marriage of their daughter
Marjorie
to
Mr Robert Blake
at Saint Fellows Church
Ringway
on Saturday 29th May
at 2.45 pm
and afterwards at a reception at
The Bullbrook Inn, Ringway

RSVP
21 Drum Lane
Ringway
Somerset
PS9 4TJ

OR

Mr and Mrs John Fowler
request the pleasure of your company
at the marriage of their daughter
Marjorie
to
Mr Robert Blake
etc.

If the number of guests is quite low, the invitation may be written by hand on suitable attractive stationery. Usually, however, they are printed. The traditional colour for the lettering is black. Write in the name of the guest or guests by hand. In the second example, the correct position is in the top left corner of the card. RSVP means 'please reply', from the French 'réspondez s'il vous plaît'.

OR

The exact wording depends on who is issuing the invitation and their relationship to the bride. For example, if the bride's parents are divorced and her mother has remained the wording could be:

Mr and Mrs William Stevens
request the pleasure of
the company of

(write in the name of the guest(s))
at the marriage of her
daughter
June Smith
etc.

Although the bride's surname is rarely included in the wording it can be appropriate where it differs from that of the host and hostess.

Reply to an invitation to a wedding (formal)

24 Tillsbury Gardens
Walthall

Mr and Mrs Peter Faulkener thank Mr and Mrs John Fowler for their kind invitation to their daughter's wedding, and to the reception, and will be most happy to attend.

OR

. . . and much regret that a prior engagement prevents them from attending.

It is not necessary to give your full address when the reply is in the nature of a brief note, so long as you establish your identity.

Invitation to a wedding (informal)

Rachel and Michael Basset

Sylvia and Andrew hope you'll join them, to celebrate their wedding at Saint Paul's Church, Littlerow, on Thursday 12th August at 1.30 pm and at a reception afterwards at the Two Drakes Restaurant, Littlerow.

RSVP
14 Cedars Close
Littlerow
Surrey
MT4 1DL

An informal invitation is most often used in the case of a second marriage or for a small wedding party of close friends.

Reply to an invitation to a wedding (informal)

Sylvia and Andrew

Thank you very much for inviting us to the wedding and reception on 12th August. Of course we will be delighted to attend.

Rachel and Michael Basset
The Tudors
Littlerow

Engagement notice in the press

The engagement is announced between Robert Blake, son of Mr and Mrs F. Blake and Marjorie, daughter of Mr and Mrs J. Fowler.

Letter announcing engagement (informal)

> 21 Drum Lane
> Ringway
> Somerset
> PS9 4TJ

Dear Auntie

I simply had to write to tell you the most marvellous news. Robert and I are engaged!

The wedding is going to be quite soon and of course we'll be sending you an invitation when we've got the time and the place sorted out.

I do hope you'll be able to come.

Love

Marjorie

Invitation to an engagement party (informal)

Rachel and Michael Basset

Sylvia and Andrew have great pleasure in inviting you to (hope you'll join them at) their engagement party at the Green Lees Hotel, Littlerow, on Saturday 24th July at 8.30 pm.

RSVP
14 Cedars Close
Littlerow
Surrey
MT4 1DL

This invitation may be written by hand and set out as shown, or printed, with the layout centred as for a formal invitation.

Reply to an invitation to an engagement party (informal)

Sylvia and Andrew

Thank you very much for inviting us to your engagement party on 24th July. Of course we will be delighted to attend.

Rachel and Michael Basset
The Tudors
Littlerow

Invitation to an engagement party (formal)

21 Drum Lane
Ringway
Somerset
PS9 4TJ

Mr and Mrs John Fowler
request the pleasure of
the company of

(write in the name of the guest(s))
at an evening party
on Saturday 14th March
at 8.30 pm
at the above address to
celebrate the engagement of their daughter
Marjorie
to
Mr Robert Blake

RSVP

An invitation such as this would usually be printed. If the party is to be at a hotel or other premises give that address in the main part of the invitation and the home address at the bottom left, under RSVP.

Reply to an invitation to an engagement party (formal)

24 Tillsbury Gardens
Walthall

Mr and Mrs Peter Faulkener have great pleasure in accepting Mr and Mrs John Fowler's invitation for Saturday, 14th March.

OR

Mr and Mrs Peter Faulkener wish to thank Mr and Mrs John Foster for their kind invitation for (to their daughter's engagement party on) Saturday 14th March and very much regret that they will be unable to attend.

Invitation to a christening

32 Bishops Avenue
Dralford
Essex
BU4 6TS

April 24th 19 -

Dear Mary

John Andrew is due to be christened on Sunday 31st April and Mark and I would love you to be there.

The christening is at 3.30 pm, and there will be a little celebration at home afterwards.

If you could arrive between 2.30 and 3.00 pm, that would be perfect.

I do hope you will be able to come.

Love

Lindsay

Reply to an invitation to a christening

109 Long Lane
Northoll
Kent
NB7 4TA

April 26th 19 -

Dear Lindsay

Thank you so much for inviting me to John Andrew's christening on Sunday. I wouldn't miss it for the world.

I should arrive by 3.00 pm, but if I'm delayed, don't wait. I'll go straight to the church.

Looking forward to seeing you and Mark again, and of course, the baby.

Love

Mary

OR

Dear Lindsay

I do hope you will forgive me when I tell you that I will not be able to make the christening on Sunday.

I am going on holiday in two days' time to Malta, and cannot change the booking now.

It was very kind of you to ask me. You know I would have loved to come.

Expect a postcard from Malta. I'll be thinking of you.

Love to John Andrew.

Mary

Invitation to an 18th birthday party (formal)

61 Tregunter Park
Lanford
Essex
NW5 2PN

Mr and Mrs Julius Seymour
request the pleasure of
the company of

(write the name of the guest(s))
at a party
on Saturday 14th December
at 8.00 pm
at the above address to
celebrate the coming of age
of their daughter
Evelyn

RSVP

Such an invitation would normally be printed. Reply as for a formal invitation to an engagement party.

Invitation to an 18th birthday party (informal)

Evelyn Seymour
has great pleasure in inviting

(write the name of the guest(s))
to her 18th birthday party
on Saturday 14th December
at 8.00 pm

RSVP
61 Tregunter Park
Lanford
Essex
NW5 2PN

This invitation may be printed as shown or written by hand and set out as in the example of an informal invitation to an engagement party. Reply in the same style also.

Invitation to a New Year's Eve party (formal)

Mr and Mrs Martin Winter
request the pleasure of

(write the name of the guest(s))
company at a
New Year's Eve Party
19 - /19 -

30 Buckland Avenue   9.00 pm
Lanford   RSVP
Essex
PT4 6HA

Reply as for an informal invitation to an engagement party. Similar wording
and layout to the examples of adult party invitations shown above may be
used for other occasions such as a wedding anniversary, house warming or
evening party.

Letter of invitation to a children's party

17 Burnside Avenue
Southam
Essex
DB2 5NX

19th December 19 -

Dear Mrs Alston

Elizabeth and David are having a few of their friends to a party
here, on Tuesday 3rd January, and hope that John will be able to
come. The party is between 4.30 and 9.00 pm.

If you are thinking of coming to fetch him, it would be nice if you
arrived at about 7.00 pm, in time for some of the fun!

Do try to manage this, as I would be very pleased to see you.

Yours sincerely

Judith Trury

This letter is, of course, written by the mother of Elizabeth and David. If
both mothers are friends, naturally only christian names would be used.

Reply to an invitation to a children's party

24 Burnside Avenue
Southam
Essex
DB2 5NX

22nd December 19 -

Dear Mrs Trury

John says 'thank you very much' for the invitation to the party on 3rd January. He is excited about it and hopes to come.

I will drop in at about 7.00 pm as you suggest, to lend a willing hand.

Looking forward to seeing you.

Yours sincerely

Lyn Alston

OR

John is most upset that he will not be able to accept the invitation for the party on 3rd January.

We are going to stay with my parents over Christmas and will be away for two weeks.

Will you please thank Elizabeth and David and tell them how sorry John is that he will not be able to come?

It was so nice of you to ask him.

Yours sincerely

Lyn Alston

Letter of invitation to a children's party (quite informal)

17 Burnside Avenue
Southam
Essex
DB2 5NX

19th December 19 -

Dear John

We are hoping to have such a lovely party on Tuesday, 3rd January, and we want you to come, as it would not be complete without you.

Write and say 'yes', please.

Love from

Elizabeth and David

4.30 - 9.00 pm

Letter of invitation to a children's party

7 Abor Close
North York
Sussex
PB5 2EG

24th February 19 -

Dear Mrs Henderson

Paul and Kathy are planning a party for Tuesday 3rd March, at about 7.30 pm, and would be very pleased if Mark could join us for the evening. Perhaps you could come too? We expect to finish at about 10.00 pm, and it would be very nice to see you.

Yours sincerely

Mary Fowler

Invitation to a children's party

Elizabeth and David Trury
are having a party
for their friends
on Tuesday 3rd January.
They sincerely hope that
Master John Alston
will be good enough to accept
this invitation
to be present.

RSVP   4.30 - 9.00 pm
17 Burnside Avenue
Southam
Essex
DB2 5NX

Most children like this formal wording as it gives the invitation an important appearance.

Invitation to dinner (formal)

Mr and Mrs James Mackie
request the pleasure of

(write the name of the guest(s))
company
at dinner on
Thursday 28th September
at 7.30 pm

RSVP
39 Fortune Park
Hartown
Cumberland
ST2 9TN

This invitation should be printed. Naturally it is reserved for very formal occasions.

Reply to a formal invitation to dinner

18 Shepherd Park
Hartown

20th September 19 -

Mr and Mrs Gerald Connor are very pleased to accept Mr and Mrs James Mackie's kind invitation to dinner on Thursday 18th September.

OR

Mr and Mrs Gerald Connor much regret that owing to a prior engagement they are unable to accept Mr and Mrs James Mackie's kind invitation to dinner on Thursday 28th September.

Letter of invitation to dinner (semi-formal)

39 Fortune Park
Hartown
Cumberland
ST2 9TN

18th September 19 -

Dear Mrs Connor

Will you and Mr Connor give us the pleasure of your company at dinner on Thursday 28th September (7.30 pm)?

We are asking a few friends, most of whom you have met before, and we very much hope that you will be able to come.

Yours sincerely

Adelaide Mackie

Reply to an invitation to dinner (semi-formal)

18 Shepherd Park
Hartown
Cumberland
ST2 7BN

20th September 19 -

Dear Mrs Mackie

Thank you very much for your kind invitation to dinner on Thursday 28th September. Gerald and I will be delighted to accept.

I need hardly tell you that we are both looking forward to seeing you.

Yours sincerely

Ann Connor

OR

Dear Mrs Mackie

Thank you very much for your kind invitation to dinner.

Unfortunately, Gerald is due to be in France on business next week and I will be visiting my sister in London, so we will not be able to be with you on 28th.

We are both very sorry. Thank you again for inviting us.

Yours sincerely

Ann Connor

Letter of invitation to dinner (informal)

39 Fortune Park
Hartown
Cumberland
ST2 9TN

18th September 19 -

Dear Ann

Please will you and Gerald come to dinner on Thursday 28th
September? We haven't seen you for ages.

There will be a few friends round, but you have met them all
before.

Now do write to say that you will be there.

Love

Adelaide

Reply to an invitation to dinner (informal)

18 Shepherd Park
Hartown
Cumberland
SJ2 7BN

20th September 19 -

Dear Adelaide

It was lovely to hear from you again. Of course Gerald and I will
be delighted to come to dinner on 28th.

We both look forward to seeing you very much.

Love

Ann

OR

Dear Adelaide

It was so nice of you to invite us to dinner on 28th — but we won't be able to make it!

Thursday is the day we've promised to be at a retirement party for one of Gerald's colleagues at work, and we can't refuse now without causing some hurt feelings.

I am sorry. You know we would have both loved to come. We must arrange another date — soon!

Love

Ann

Letter of invitation to stay with the writer

38 Blessops Drive
Stambury
Wiltshire
WP6 6DX

19th May 19 -

Dear Rowan

William and I are quite worried that we haven't heard from you recently.

When we saw you last year you said you might be coming to England sometime in the summer. Why not come now? We would love to see you and you can stay here for a couple of weeks. The spare room is decorated and ready, and you must see how the garden is coming on.

If you can come for a while, let us know when and William can take some days off work.

Do write soon and say yes.

Love

Patricia and William

Reply to invitation to stay

20 Ruby Road
Kirkthorn
Ayrshire
TF1 2PD

21st May 19 -

Dear Patricia and William

How nice to hear from you.

I'm sorry that I have not been in touch before. I never was one for writing letters as you know.

It's good to know that you are both obviously well, and marvellous to think that you are willing to put up with me for a couple of weeks.

Actually, I will be be in your part of the country next month at a conference in Oxford. It begins on 23rd, and I will be there for three days.

I would love to see you both after that. If I arrived on Monday 27th during the afternoon would that be all right? I can make my own way from the station.

See you soon

Rowan

Invitation to stay at Christmas

The Glens
Mapel Road
Havenworth
Kent
SN3 2DS

10th December 19 -

Dear Uncle Robert

We all want you to come and help us enjoy Christmas this year. Will you come on 23rd and stay for the New Year?

The children are looking forward to seeing you again — and some more of your stories about life at sea!

We shall be having a fairly quiet Christmas, but mother and father will be over on Boxing Day and I expect we will have some good long walks in the country. The weather is lovely and crisp.

Having you to stay will make it just perfect, so please don't think of refusing.

Love

Anne

Reply to an invitation to stay at Christmas

29 Albany Road
Bathton
Devon
PS9 4TQ

13th December 19 -

Dear Anne

It was very nice of you to think of inviting me for Christmas. It would be lovely to see you, Mark and the children again.

I shall take you up on your offer then, and arrive on 23rd. Prepare to be bored by a host of old sea yarns!

Your affectionate uncle

Robert

OR

Unfortunately, I have already promised to play host this year. An old friend is coming over from Canada and will be staying for several weeks.

Much as I'd have loved to come, therefore, I am afraid I won't be able to make it this time.

Please give the children my love, and tell them I hope to see them soon.

Thank you again for inviting me.

Your affectionate uncle

Robert

Invitation to a dance (formal)

The T R A Company
has pleasure in inviting

(write the name of the guest(s))
to their annual dinner and dance
at Forton Hotel
Blissop
on Saturday 4th December
at 7.30 pm

RSVP   Dress formal
The Secretary
T R A House
Blissop
Norfolk
XT8 4JM

Reply to an invitation to a dance (formal)

2 Farmers Walk
Bantham

Mr and Mrs Leonard Foster have great pleasure in accepting the invitation to a dinner and dance on 4th December.

OR

Mr and Mrs Leonard Foster regret that due to a prior engagement they are unable to accept the invitation to a dinner and dance on 4th December.

Letter of thanks after a holiday

20 Rugby Road
Kirkthorn
Ayrshire
TF1 2PD

10th June 19 -

Dear Patricia and William

I just had to write to tell you how much I enjoyed my stay with you both. I am full of admiration for the way you have tackled the house and garden, and Patricia, your cooking was a delight!

Remember, now you owe me a visit, and thanks again.

Rowan

Letter of thanks after a party (adult)

14 Weybone Park
Wellend
Lancashire
LC2 6BH

14th March 19 -

Dear Susan

Alan and I really enjoyed the party last week and this is just to say thank you for inviting us!

It was great fun. How about having a party every week?

Love

Katie

Letter of thanks after a party (children's)

24 Trewin Avenue
Brimbley
Cheshire
WA7 6TN

18th August 19 -

Dear Mrs Ulston

I thought I'd just write to say thank you very much for inviting David to the party last week.

He hasn't stopped talking about all the games he played and the presents he won! It sounds as if all the children had a wonderful time.

Thank you again for having David. I hope he wasn't too much of a handful!

Yours sincerely

Margaret Birdham

Letter of thanks for a present (adult)

19 Fins Way
Belberry
Wiltshire
WXP 2DF

28th December 19 -

Dear William

Thank you very much for your letter and the beautiful silk scarf.
They arrived just in time for Christmas.

Green is one of my favourite colours so you may rest assured that
I will make good use of the scarf.

I do hope that you will be able to come home for Christmas next
year. You know I like to keep in touch with all my nephews and it
would be so nice to see you again.

Love

Auntie Jane

Letter of thanks for a present (child)

17 Cherry Close
Downfield
Yorkshire
EN2 6DP

15th July 19 -

Dear Uncle George

Thank you very much for sending me the Sherlock Holmes book
for my birthday.

Mummy and daddy bought me a watch and I got lots of other
presents but yours is one of the nicest. I'm really enjoying reading
it.

Love

James

LOVE, COURTSHIP AND MARRIAGE

Love letters are the most highly personal of all forms of correspondence and it would be misleading to try to lay down rules for this sort of writing. The best thing is simply to *be yourself*. Do not aim for a highly literary style or your letters will look artificial. Try to write as you would talk to your loved one. It's not the layout or the grammatical excellence that counts, but the sincerity of your feeling.

The normal rules for beginning and ending letters do not apply to love letters. Although *Dearest James, Darling Sandra,* or simply *Darling* are often used, originality — when it's not merely being clever — is half the charm of a love letter. Similarly with the ending. You can hardly leave out the word love altogether, but the exact wording is entirely up to you.

It is, however, best not to overdo endearments such as kisses or hearts, or they will lose their value. Do not put X's or cryptic messages on the backs of envelopes. Whoever receives the letter will probably not thank you for letting everyone, including the postman, know about the relationship.

The letters that follow can only show one style of writing a love letter. If they sound 'wrong' to you, don't use them. At best, they are merely a framework for your own personal sentiments.

Love letter from a man

3 Brent Walk
Hanorten
Middlesex
TW2 5KL

18th June 19 -

Dearest Lisa

Monday again — and another long week to go before I'll see you again. It seems more like a year to me!

I'm writing this in the rest room at break, but somehow it doesn't feel as if I'm really back at work at all. I'm still thinking about all the things we said and did at the weekend.

I'll have to work late on Thursday and Friday. Maybe it will make the time go faster, although I think even if I could see you every day it wouldn't be enough!

I'll have to go now darling. I'm getting 'back to work' looks from Dunnerton.

Write soon — and remember, I love you.

Martin

Reply to love letter from a man

13 Ockwood Road
Pinnault
Sussex
GX7 6DP

20th June 19 -

Dear Martin

Your letter arrived this morning. I saw the postman halfway down the road and decided to hang on, hoping. I was right.

I read it (three times) on the way into work, and got so absorbed that the half hour journey seemed no time at all. I didn't notice all those usual boring stops!

At lunch time I sat in the park, trying to encourage my tan, and wished it was Saturday instead of Wednesday.

Last night I dreamed we were walking along a deserted beach and swimming in the sea; it must be all those holiday brochures we were looking at the other day.

Love is . . . hanging on for the postman when you're late for work already!

Love and kisses

Lisa

Love letter from a man following a parting

Camp 4
Marxus Oil Field
Gulf City
New Arabia

7th September 19 -

Ann Darling

It seems for ever since I was with you in England, instead of just three weeks. Do you miss me as much as I miss you?

Everyone is being very helpful but I just wish you could be over here, too. Remember when you said it didn't matter how far apart we were, you would never stop loving me? Well, that's the way I feel right now.

I'm working as many hours as the firm will allow, and I've already got quite a bit saved up. When I come home on leave, we can go to the best restaurant in town!

They have a saying out here — everything comes to those who wait. I think that must be me, for as far as I'm concerned, you *are* everything.

Your loving

Terry

Reply to a love letter following a parting

17 Hillhead Gardens
Romside
Kent
MP2 7JA

9th September 19 -

Dearest Terry

Your letter arrived on Saturday and cheered me up enormously. Weekends are so dull when you're not here.

I'm glad to hear you are working hard and able to earn some extra money — although I'd rather have you back with me. I wouldn't mind missing out on the best restaurant in town. Anyway, I

43

thought my kitchen was the best in the world — that's what you said!

I am enclosing a photograph I had taken in a studio last week. I hope you like it. I tried to look all dreamy and romantic but it's not that easy when you're rushing around in the lunch hour. Can you send me one of you, outside your camp?

I miss you so very much.

Lots of love

Ann

Letter from a man after a quarrel (1)

26 Portland Street
West Winsloe
Cornwall
TB7 2FM

2nd February 19 -

Dearest Patricia

We always agreed to be honest with each other so I'm not going to pretend to be a penitent sinner now, because I don't feel like one.

I thought you were unfair to be so angry with me. I still think so, but I realise I didn't help matters by the way I reacted.

I don't mind admitting that I've been feeling pretty fed up since our row. I badly want to see you again, but I don't suppose you would think much of me if I tried to make up by saying it was all my fault. I reckon it was about fifty fifty and I just hope you'll agree to forget the whole thing ever happened.

Darling I love you as much as I ever did. When can I come round and see you again?

Much love

Peter

Letter from a man after a quarrel (2)

19 Winner Park
Norbalton
Hertfordshire
HP6 4MN

18th May 19 -

Dear Rachel

Will you forgive — and forget?

I don't know how or why I could have said what I did and I am
furious with myself for being such a fool.

This is the first time that we have quarrelled and I am determined
that it will be the last. I've never felt so miserable in my life.

When may I come round and see you again?

All my love

John

Reply to a letter after a quarrel

20 Aitken Gardens
Norbalton
Hertfordshire
HP4 3JT

19th May 19 -

Dear John

It's already forgotten. And as far as I am concerned, there's
nothing to forgive. We both said things in the heat of the moment
which we didn't mean.

The best part of breaking up is supposed to be making up — so
please come round as soon as you can and let's make up.

I love you

Rachel

Proposals for marriage

Proposals for marriage are almost always made verbally. The reasons are obvious. Even a stammered proposal is more likely to be favourably received than a beautifully written letter. If you write because you fear rejection you will probably have your fear confirmed!

A proposal should be made by letter only when there are special circumstances that make a verbal proposal impracticable — usually when there is a long distance between the two parties. If it is impossible to overcome this — as it may be, for example, in the case of military service or overseas employment — then a letter is justified.

Courtship by correspondence is best done gradually; a proposal should be led up to in previous letters. The form of the proposal will depend a great deal on what has been said before, but the important thing is that there should be no noticeable change of style. The following letter should be read with that in mind.

Letter from a man proposing marriage

1007 Milkanny Walk
Southern Precinct
Milkanny
Ontario
Canada

1st March 19 -

Darling

You must know how much I miss you and want to be with you. I've told you so many times in my letters to you before — and my love for you just gets stronger with each day we're apart.

Perhaps if I were home I could say this letter, but I can't put it off any longer. So here it is; darling, will you marry me?

I know I can't offer you much, and I don't even know how long I'll be stuck out here. But it can't be for much longer, and the waiting will be less unbearable if I can think that the end will be the beginning of a new life with you.

Darling, if this sounds clumsy and contrived, it's because it isn't easy to express feelings like this in a letter. I only hope you can read between the lines and guess just how much I really love and want you.

You have . . . all my love

Don

Letter postponing an answer to a proposal of marriage

29 Graves Lane
Ostlewood
Kent
BN7 5DE

4th March 19 -

Dearest Don

I was very flattered to receive your letter and the proposal —
although I must admit, it took me rather by surprise.

Don, you know that I care for you very much. I really do. But I
honestly don't know whether I love you enough to marry you. I
didn't know you for very long when you were in England, and I
won't really know how I feel until I see you again.

I know it's unsatisfactory not to say clearly 'yes' or 'no', but
marriage is such a big step that I think we just need more time
together before making a decision.

Perhaps you will find that I'm not quite all you imagine now you
can't seè me. I should hate you to come back and find that you
didn't love your fiancée after all!

Don, if you are willing to wait to see how it works out, I am too. I
still haven't met anyone half as nice as you. If I didn't truly believe
that it was the best way for both of us, I would never take this risk
of losing. you.

Please write soon

Love

Edwina

Letter accepting a proposal of marriage

29 Graves Lane
Ostlewood
Kent
BN7 5DE

4th March 19 -

Dear darling Don

Yes — but yes, of course I will marry you.

But that is just to confirm my telegram with the same message which you should get today or tomorrow. This air mail is too slow for me!

I have told Mother and Father and of course they are tremendously pleased. You know they always did approve of you.

Now I can hardly wait until you're home. The weeks seem to pass so slowly; it's quite unbearable. Perhaps I should turn my mind to 'marriage plans' — the ring, the wedding, the honeymoon, the house. You see, I'm getting quite carried away!

Seriously Don, I miss you like crazy. Write soon. I'm dreaming of you all the time.

All my love

Edwina

Letter not accepting a proposal of marriage

29 Graves Lane
Ostlewood
Kent
BN7 5DE

4th March 19 -

Dearest Don

You have paid me the greatest compliment any girl can receive and the least I can do is to give you my answer promptly and frankly. Don, I care very much about you — but I'm afraid the answer is no.

It would be easy for me to say that we didn't know each other well enough or that I'm not sure about my feelings towards you. But that would be untrue.

Please don't take it too much to heart when I tell you that although I like and admire you tremendously, I'm not in love with you — and I never shall be.

Don, I'm not worth your regrets. I've risked hurting your feelings because I don't want you to go on wasting your hopes on me. And I know you'll find someone much better fitted to be your wife than I am.

I hope you will understand, and will always think of me as,

Your very good friend

Edwina

Letter breaking off an engagement/relationship (1)

21 Merryfield Park
Fulverton
Hampshire
TN3 9BE

19th April 19 -

Dear Ian

Your letter arrived this morning. It was so nice, that it makes what I've got to say sound awful. It's not meant to be.

Ian, I think that for some time we've both been pretending to each other. Maybe we were in love at first and if so, I don't know how or why it changed, but I know now that although I'm very fond of you, I can never really love you properly.

It's painful for me to write this and it's taken a long time to put pen to paper. But I'm sure you will agree it's best to be honest.

We're bound to see each other again and I hope that when we do, we can still be very good friends.

Yours sincerely

Laura

This letter could equally well be written by a man.

Letter breaking off an engagement/relationship (2)

36 Ditton Lane
Charmap
Devon
WP2 7LB

11th July 19 -

Dear Harry

That unfortunate incident last Saturday is, I feel, just the latest in a series of incidents which show that it would be pointless to continue our relationship.

Please do not think that I am simply blaming you. For some weeks I have felt that we were drifting apart.

We have had a lot of good times together which I will remember with fondness, but our futures, I am sure, lie in different directions.

Harry, I still think of you as a friend, and I hope that you will be able to think the same of me.

Yours sincerely

Ruth

Letter breaking off an engagement/relationship (3)

12 Charlesworth
Place
Mepham
Middlesex
MB2 7H4

2nd October 19 -

Dear Jim

I must thank you for your letter. Unfortunately I cannot reconsider my decision. It was final.

Yours sincerely

Elizabeth

Letter breaking off an engagement/relationsip (4)

12 Charlesworth
Place
Mepham
Middlesex
MB2 7H4

28th September 19 -

Dear Jim

In all the circumstances I have no choice but to break off our
engagement (relationship). It would be futile to go over all the
reasons for this decision as it would only serve to hurt us both.
Please do not make this any harder than it is by raking over old
arguments. I am sure this is the right decision for us both.

Yours sincerely

Elizabeth

Brevity, not pages of recrimination, is often the best way to end a relationship
which is clearly not working.

Letter of congratulation to a girlfriend on her engagement

14 Acacia Lane
Widmouth
Shropshire
SF10 2DE

23rd March 19 -

Dearest Mary

I was so pleased to hear the news of your engagement that I just
had to write to say congratulations — to you and of course to
David. I always thought you made a lovely couple, and I am sure
you will be very happy together.

Now you must come and tell me what plans you both have for the
future. I'm dying to know all about it.

Love

Jean

Letter of congratulation to a mother on her daughter's engagement

17 Middens Way
Bestwood
Surrey
PN7 6YD

23rd March 19 -

Dear Celia

May I as an old friend send you my congratulations on Mary's engagement to David which I saw announced in the paper yesterday.

You must be very pleased. David and Mary seem such a suited young couple that I'm sure you need have no fears for their future happiness.

Do give my love and very best wishes to Mary.

With kindest regards from John and myself.

Yours sincerely

Margaret Roberts

Letter of thanks for a wedding present

9 Ferndale Street
Rhyde
Surrey
PR6 2DS

14th August 19 -

Dear Auntie Mabel

How kind of you and Uncle James to send us such a lovely coffee set as a wedding present. You may be sure it will see plenty of use once David and I are settled in our new home.

We are looking forward to having you with us at the wedding. I hope you will both come to see us after the honeymoon — and find out just how good the coffee really is!

Yours affectionately

Mary

Letter of congratulations on a silver wedding anniversary

20 Newmede Road
East Renich
Dorset
DB7 4PX

17th November 19 -

Dear Tom

It's just 25 years tomorrow since I proposed a toast to a smiling groom and his lovely bride and wished them a long and happy life together.

My wishes were well founded. You and Geraldine have every right to feel pleased with yourselves. I know of only one other couple who have been as happy together as you — and you can probably guess who I mean!

Ann joins me in wishing you many more years of happiness together. We enclose a little memento of the occasion — and I hope that we shall be able to send you another one in gold in 25 years' time.

Yours sincerely

Chris

Acknowledgement to a letter of congratulation on a silver wedding anniversary

52 Webster Park
Middenport
Essex
NB3 1HB

19th November 19 -

Dear Chris

It was very kind of you to think of Geraldine and myself on our silver wedding anniversary.

We were absolutely delighted with your letter and the lovely Wedgwood vase which is now filled with flowers and has pride of place on the dining room table.

It really was a very nice gesture indeed, and one which Geraldine and I look forward to reciprocating next year when you join us in this silvered respectability.

Our thanks and very best wishes to you and Ann.

Yours sincerely

Tom

Letter asking a friend to be best man at a wedding

14a South Street
Bullerton
Cornwall
GB1 6FL

3rd June 19 -

Dear Gerry

Joanne and I have now fixed the date of our wedding for Saturday 24th August, and I would be tremendously pleased if you would agree to be the best man.

I know it might be a bit difficult because of the distance involved, but if you can arrange to come down I would be delighted to put you up for a few days before the wedding. With your powers of organisation and oratory the ceremony itself should be no problem at all!

If you can't make it I will understand — but I must insist that you attend the wedding at least!

It would be marvellous to see you again, so do write and tell me you'll do it.

Yours sincerely

Dave

Letter asking a friend to be chief bridesmaid at a wedding

19 Norry Drive
Amblenney
Kent
P27 2WR

7th May 19 -

Dear Alison

I'm writing to ask if you will do me the most tremendous favour. Will you be my chief bridesmaid at the wedding?

Alan and I have set the date for 3rd July and of course you could stay for a week or so before the 'big day'. It would be lovely to see you again. There's so much to tell you.

Now do write and say yes. I just cannot think of anyone I'd rather have with me when we march up the aisle!

Love

Kathy

Normally a best man or a chief bridesmaid would live nearer to the groom or bride and the offer would be made verbally. However, if it is not clear that the offer will be accepted, as when considerable distances are involved, a letter frees the recipient from too much pressure to say yes, and avoids what could be an embarrassing situation should the answer be no.

APPOINTMENTS

When writing to a prospective employer, it is important to remember that the letter will be your ambassador. It will create an impression of you in the mind of the recipient on the basis of which he will decide whether or not to pursue your application. Obviously you must write, or type, your letter neatly, laying it out according to the conventions described in Chapter One. You should include all the *relevant* information, but avoid unnecessary details; remember that the person you are writing to is probably busy. Do not be afraid to let your character show through your letter, but try not to become chatty.

If you are applying for a post which may involve typing, the letter should be typed as a perfect example of your skill. In other cases a neatly written letter will create a better impression than a badly typed one, but a well typed letter would be better still.

Letters involving a refusal or rejection are often awkward to write. It is important to be firm, but never rude or harsh, and while it is often helpful to give your reasons, white lies are normally best avoided.

In all cases, decide what you want to say before you start writing; write as simply and clearly as possible, and avoid clichés and pompous language which you would not use in ordinary speech.

Curriculum vitae in general

The object of a curriculum vitae (sometimes abbreviated to c.v.) is to set out the bare details of your education, employment and personal status as a reference or quick guide for the person who requested it. You should always include your name, address and date of birth, and it is normal to give the names and addresses of two referees (i.e. persons the recipient can refer to regarding your status). Your c.v. is not the place to write a descriptive essay; just state the facts. It should be written on a separate sheet of paper, enclosed with an explanatory letter, and should be as clearly laid out as possible.

Curriculum vitae (1)

Name: Jane Brown
Address: 43 Chalcot Park
London
NW1 6AX
Telephone: home 485 0396
office 822 3065
Date of birth: October 7th 1960
Marital status: single
Secondary education: St Mark's School
Edgware
Middlesex
TP4 3SZ
1971 - 1977
3 CSE   English Language
Mathematics
Geography
2 'O' levels Art
English Literature
Employment: Clerical Assistant with Jones Bros Ltd, Tower Road,
London N1 2ER, 1978 - date.
Referees: Mr S Colins
Jones Bros Ltd
Tower Road
London N1 2ER

Mrs R Smith
Headmistress
St Mark's School
Edgware
Middlesex
TP4 3SZ

Curriculum vitae (2)

Name: John Smith
Address: 69 Lower Terrace
Onsworth
Bedfordshire
DF7 2SJ
Telephone: home Onsworth 638006
office Onsworth 534662
Date of birth: 8th August 1948
Marital status: married
Education since 11:   Penworthy Grammar School
Penworthy
Bedfordshire
FT2 6PN
1959 - 66
6 'O' levels
3 'A' levels   History Grade B
Geography Grade C
Latin Grade C
Manchter University
1966 - 69
BA (History) Second Class Hons.
Employment: Management Trainee with Unitech Limited, Unitech House, Queen St, Onsworth DB6 6TZ , 1970 - 71; promoted to Assistant Manager (sales) 1971 - 75; Area Manager (marketing) with Framley (UK) Ltd, Hope House, Thorpe Way, Onsworth DJ2 2PT, 1975 - date.
Referees: Mr K Park
Faculty of Arts
Manchter University
Manchter
FP6 2NP

Mr B Crane
Managing Director
Framley (UK) Ltd
Hope House
Thorpe Way
Onsworth
DJ2 2PT

Applications on 'spec'

As with any other job application, an enquiry written 'on spec' must create a good impression on its reader. You will naturally speak of your own abilities, qualifications and experience, but it is also important to say why you think these would be useful to your reader's organisation.

If you would be willing and able to do various jobs, make this clear; but never try to impress by claiming to be able to do things which you cannot in fact manage. Say what jobs you really think you can handle, and at what level.

It is a good plan to find out something about the organisation you are writing to, and then to use what you have discovered in your letter in order to show that you have taken some trouble. If possible, find out the name of the personnel officer or staff manager, and write to him or her in person.

Application on spec for a position as junior office assistant

18 Field Gardens
Brimton
Bedfordshire
AB6 5PR

7th February 19 -

J Bloggs and Sons Limited
5 Queen's Crescent
Brimton
Bedfordshire
MB4 PQ8

Dear Sir

I am writing to enquire whether you have any vacancies for a junior office assistant.

I left King Edward's School last Christmas, having passed CSE Examinations in English Language, Geography and French. In my last year at school I also took a course in typing and general office procedures, and I am keen to make proper use of these skills.

Since leaving school I have not been able to find a regular job, but I have done some temporary work with Messrs Smith and Jones, who have been pleased with my work. Mr Smith has himself assured me that he will be quite willing to give me a favourable reference.

I realise that you may not have any vacancies at present, but I would be very willing to work in any department and to undertake any training required. I therefore hope that you will consider my application favourably whenever a possible position arises.

Yours faithfully

Caroline Brown (Miss)

Application on spec for a position in a sales department

9 Thorpe Way
Farnworth
London
W8 6FH

10th July 19 -

K Crane Esq
Personnel Officer
Maplock (UK) Limited
Maplock House
Lower Road
London
W6X 5PJ

Dear Mr Crane

I am writing to enquire whether you may have any vacancies, at an executive level, in your Sales Department. James Brown, who is a mutual acquaintance, suggested that I write to you because he tells me that your firm is expanding in this area just now.

As you will see from the enclosed curriculum vitae, I have a sound educational background, and several years' experience in the sales departments of two well known firms. Whilst employed with Tailor Marketing I also gained valuable experience as a salesman 'on the road'.

You may have heard that Thorpe & Co. Ltd are closing down at the end of September, and it is for this reason that I was made redundant last month. I am very anxious not to remain without work for long, and am quite willing to consider any post for which you think I may be suitable.

Yours sincerely

John Bone

Application for a position as a secretary/typist

24 York Road
Cartown
Yorks
LM6 2RZ

10th July 19 -

Crumb & Cake Limited
154-158 Church Way
Cartown
Yorks
SL8 5RC

Dear Sir

I am writing in answer to your advertisement in this week's *Cartown Chronicle* for a secretary/typist.

I am twenty-one years old, and was educated at Mallow Comprehensive where I obtained CSE passes in English Language, French, Mathematics, Domestic Science and Typing.

For the past two years I have been working in the Personnel Department of J. Jones and Sons, as a junior shorthand-typist. My speeds are 100 wpm for shorthand and 60 wpm for typing.

Although I enjoy my present job, I am keen to broaden my experience, and to find a post with a little more responsibility.

My Departmental Manager, Mr Brian Lovell, has agreed to give me time off to come for an interview on any afternoon other than Thursdays, and is also willing to write a reference.

Yours faithfully

Susan Brown

Application for a position as a salesman

Hollydene
Collingwood Road
Nanton
Bedfordshire
SL5 6XC

10th August 19 -

Box 3998
The Daily Mercury
156 Hope Lane
London
EC3 7YP

Dear Sirs

I am writing in answer to your advertisement in today's *Daily Mercury* for a Sales Representative.

I have had seven years' experience of the type of selling you outline, starting as a trainee with ILC Ltd, and progressing to my present position of Area Sales Representative (South-east) with Jones Brothers of Dunstable. I am now keen to advance my career in a larger organisation with opportunities to engage in overseas selling techniques.

I enclose my curriculum vitae, including the names of two referees. If my qualifications interest you, I should be happy to come for an interview at any time convenient to you.

Yours faithfully

Colin Brown

Enc

Application for a position as a motor mechanic

55 Davidson Avenue
Manchter
FP7 7TS

14th September 19 -

Mr H Ody
The Apsley Motor Company
Jowett Road
Manchter
MN3 1AK

Dear Mr Ody

I wish to apply for the position of skilled motor mechanic advertised in today's *Manchter Gazette*.

Having completed a full apprenticeship, I have been employed by Jones Motors in the London Road for the past two years. I am now anxious to move to a firm where there are greater prospects for promotion and more interesting work, which is why I am applying for your vacancy.

My present manager, Mr Brian, has agreed to give me a good reference, and I would be free to come for an interview any evening after 4.30 pm.

Yours sincerely

John Collins

In the previous three examples the applicant is already in employment. In such cases it is a good idea to explain why you want to change your job in case anyone believe you are leaving at your employer's behest.

Application for a position as a clerical officer

66 Windsor Avenue
Westlea
Northley
WJ2 6DS

18th September 19 -

J. Braid
Sales Director
Messrs F R Sims and Sons Limited
Friary Road
Northley
WJ4 1SX

Dear Sir

I am writing in answer to your advertisement for a Senior Clerical Officer, which was advertised in last Friday's *Evening Post*.

I am thirty years of age, unmarried and in good health. I was educated at St Anne's Convent, Northley, where I obtained four GCE 'O' levels in English Language, History, Geography and Mathematics. I then went to Northley Polytechnic where I took a course in office procedures and business methods. After various temporary posts I secured a position as Junior Clerical Officer at Smith & Jones Limited, York Way, Northley, where I stayed for ten years. During that time I was promoted to Senior Ledger Clerk, a post I held until the firm was closed last year. I am now doing temporary work again but am very anxious to find secure employment, and I hope you will look favourably on my application.

I would be able to come for an interview at any time, but would much appreciate three days notice for the convenience of the agency whose books I am currently on. I can provide excellent references should you so wish.

Yours faithfully

Caroline Brown

Application for a position as a computer programmer

68 Courtwood Road
Horfield
London
N8 5RP

16th March 19 -

Personnel Officer
Perry Computers Limited
18-22 Milton Close
Milton Trading Estate
London
N19 6XJ

Dear Sir

I would like to apply for the post of Computer Programmer which was advertised in the 9th March issue of *Computer Weekly.*

I enclose my curriculum vitae, from which you will see that I have a good educational background, together with seven years of experience as a Computer Programmer. During my five years with Brown and Company I have gained experience of a wide variety of programmes and techniques, including the new beta software system. I would now like to further my career by specialising in the fields which your advertisement mentions.

I would be happy to come for an interview at any time.

Yours faithfully

John Smith

Enc

There is no need to go into detail about your work experience and qualifications providing your c.v. covers these adequately.

Application for a position as an export manager

15 Oakfield Drive
Briarley
W11 6XG

29th June 19 -

The Secretary
The Empire Trading Company
Ships Wharf
Briarley
EC3 8LM

Dear Sir

I am writing in answer to your advertisement, in Saturday's *Times,* for an Export Manager.

I have had eight years' experience in the export departments of two large organisations, starting as a trainee and earning promotion to my present position of Assistant Sales Manager in charge of exports. During the last three years I have been responsible for finding and expanding new markets in the Far East and South America, and I feel that this experience would enable me to undertake full responsibility for your Export Department.

I enclose a curriculum vitae, together with the addresses of two referees, my present Managing Director Mr John Wills, and Mr James Booth who supervised my training at the Far Eastern Trading Company.

I will be pleased to give you any further information you may need, and to come for an interview at any convenient time. I should mention, however, that I will be out of the country on business from 16th - 24th July; I hope that this will not inconvenience you.

Yours faithfully

Harry Binns

Enc

Application for a position as a solicitor

15 Lindhurst Gardens
Old Polesford
Hants
SL6 8RY

16th October 19 -

Messrs Jones Smith Brown & Brown
12 King's Road
Farleigh
Hants
1SB 4DD

Dear Sirs

I read your advertisement for a Litigation Solicitor in the *Law Journal* of 10th October, and would like to be considered for the position.

As you will see from the enclosed curriculum vitae, I have been working for Polesford District Council for the past five years. During that time I have been involved in all forms of litigation work and have gained considerable experience of advocacy in county, magistrates and juvenile courts. I would now like to put this experience to work in private practice, particularly with a firm such as yours which specialises in criminal cases, an area of the law which I find especially rewarding and interesting.

I would be glad to come for an interview, but know you will understand that appearances in court make it impossible for me to be free at all times. I hope very much that this will not present any serious inconvenience to you.

Yours faithfully

Miles Cox

Enc

Letter requesting applicant to attend an interview

Messrs Jones Smith
Brown & Brown
12 King's Road
Farleigh
Hants
1SB 4DD

Mr M Cox
15 Lindhurst Gardens
Old Polesford
Hants
SL6 8RY

20th October 19 -

Dear Mr Cox

My partners and I were most interested in your application for our position of Litigation Solicitor.

We would like to meet you to discuss the position further, and I would therefore be glad if you would telephone my secretary, Miss Allcock, to arrange an appointment as soon as possible.

Yours sincerely
Messrs Jones Smith Brown & Brown

Michael Jones

Letter in reply to a request for an interview

25 Oakley Avenue
Milton
Northants
WR6 9SZ

16th May 19 -

J George Esq
Kingley Marketing
64 King Street
Milton
Northants
SY7 8PL

Dear Mr George

Thank you very much for your letter of 13th May. I would be

happy to come for an interview on 21st May at 2.00 pm, and will bring with me the two references you request.

Yours sincerely

Brian Butts

It is important to send a letter in this situation not merely as a confirmation that you will attend, but also to show that you are taking the matter seriously and pay attention to detail.

Letter offering employment

Messrs Jones Smith
Brown & Brown
12 King's Road
Farleigh
Hants
1SB 4DD

4th November 19 -

Mr M Cox
15 Lindhurst Gardens
Old Polesford
Hants
SL6 8RY

Dear Mr Cox

I am delighted to tell you that my partners and I have decided to offer you the post of Litigation Solicitor with our firm.

Since you told me that you must give one month's notice to your present employers, it would seem sensible for you not to take up your position here until 2nd January next. I have entered this date on the enclosed contract of employment, which I would ask you to sign and return to me as soon as possible.

I hope you will enjoy working at Jones Smith Brown & Brown.

Yours sincerely
Jones Smith Brown & Brown

Michael Jones

Enc

Letter accepting an offer of employment

9 Poole Road
Oxridge
Bucks
SL9 6TB

15th October 19 -

R Burns Esq
Personnel Manager
Timetec Limited
Rose Estate
Oxridge
Bucks
SL9 5RF

Dear Mr Burns

Thank you for your letter of 12th October offering me the post of Ledger Clerk with your organisation.

I am delighted to accept the position and look forward to starting work with you on 15th November.

Yours sincerely

Jane Allcock

Letter not accepting an offer of employment

9 Poole Road
Oxridge
Bucks
SL9 6TB

R Burns Esq
Personnel Manager
Timetec Limited
Rose Estate
Oxridge
Bucks
SL9 5RF

15th October 19 -

Dear Mr Burns

Thank you very much for your letter of 12th October offering me the post of Ledger Clerk with your organisation.

I am afraid that after much careful thought I have decided that I cannot accept the position. As I explained when we met, I am really looking for a job with greater possibilities for broadening my experience in the accountancy field, and I have now been offered just such a post.

I hope that my decision will not inconvenience you, and I would like to thank you for your confidence in my abilities.

Yours sincerely

Jane Allcock

Letter rejecting an application

Timetec Limited
Rose Estate
Oxridge
Bucks
SL9 5RF

13th October 19 -

Miss J Allcock
9 Poole Road
Oxridge
Bucks
SL9 6TB

Dear Miss Allcock

I am afraid that after careful consideration I have decided that I cannot offer you the position of Ledger Clerk.

You undoubtedly have considerable ability but, as I explained at your interview, we are looking for someone with rather more experience.

Thank you very much for your time in attending for interview.

Yours sincerely
Timetec Limited

Roger Burns

Letter applying to be a mail order agent

344 York Drive
Manhead
Yorks
DT6 9IJ

5th June 19 -

Shuttleforth and Company
Shuttleforth House
Morton Way
Paley
Devon
DR6 9OP

Dear Sirs

I am writing to enquire about the possibility of becoming one of
your catalogue agents.

An old friend of mine, Mrs J. Jones, has been selling for you for
the past five years, and speaks very highly of your goods. I
understand that you have an application form for prospective
agents, and would be grateful if you could send me one.

Yours faithfully

Brenda Bloggs (Mrs)

Letter asking for a reference (from applicant)

15 Greenland Road
Povey
Dorset
MR2 7YT

23rd August 19 -

M Deacon Esq
Timber Products Limited
Poolford
Dorset
YT7 9IJ

Dear Mr Deacon

I am applying for the post of Works Manager at the Royal Oak
Timber Company, Markyate, and wonder whether you would allow
me to give your name as a referee.

Although I have always been very happy working at Timber Products, my wife and I would like to move nearer to her family now that our baby is on the way.

If my application is not successful, I hope that you will not feel I am in any way dissatisfied with my job here. The move would be entirely for personal reasons.

Yours sincerely

James Long

Always tell the people whom you are naming as referees, even if you are quite certain that they will not mind.

Letter following up a reference (from an employer)

Kingley Marketing
64 King Street
Milton
Northants
SY7 8PL

23rd May 19 -

B Brown Esq
M & B Creative Marketing
Dower House
Porton
Northants
RT6 3ER

Dear Mr Brown

Mr Brian Butts, of 25 Oakley Avenue, Milton, has applied to me for the post of Salesman. I understand that he was employed by you for four years in a similar capacity. He has put your name forward as a referee, and I would be most grateful if you would let me know whether you found him capable and totally reliable. I am particularly concerned to know whether, in your experience, he is able to work independently on his own initiative. It goes without saying that whatever you tell me will be treated in the strictest confidence.

I am enclosing a stamped addressed envelope for your reply.

Yours sincerely
Kingley Marketing

John George

It is always best to send letters of reference to a named individual, and to mark the envelope 'Confidential'.

If you are asked to provide a reference by someone whom you feel you cannot recommend, it is best to refuse politely at the outset. However, if you *have* to write a reference for such a person, you should state the fact that you have reservations, while trying to avoid any specific accusations.

Writing a favourable reference is much easier, but remember to keep your recommendation relevant to the nature of the job applied for.

Letter of reference

Timber Products
Limited
Dorset
YT7 9IJ

30th August 19 -

Personnel Manager   Our ref. MD/JL
Royal Oak Timber Company
Markyate   Your ref. PR7/8/82
RT6 9OK

Dear Sir

In reply to your request for information about James Long, who has applied for the position of Works Manager with your company, I can confirm he has been an employee at this company for eight years.

He served a two year apprenticeship with us, and a year later was promoted to line foreman. He has always shown himself to be a hard worker and is a popular member of our workforce. Last year we put his managerial skills to the test with promotion to Assistant Works Manager, and we found our decision to be fully justified.

Mr Long is an honest and reliable person and has, I believe, the initiative, experience and capabilities to handle the job for which he has applied.

If you require any further information please do not hesitate to get in touch with me.

Yours faithfully
Royal Oak Timber Company

Michael Deacon
Managing Director

Letter of resignation

15 Thames Mews
Malford
Berks
JU9 4RF

14th July 19 -

M Broad Esq
Personnel Manager
Flight and Pearce Limited
Malford
Berks
YO9 3PM

Dear Mr Broad

I am writing to inform you that I have been offered the position of Chief Buyer with Smith and Allsopp of 19 High Street, and I have accepted the post since it will give me greater responsibility and an increased salary.

I would like to take this opportunity to say how much I have enjoyed working at Flight and Pearce. Nevertheless I feel that I owe it to myself and my family to further my career by making this move, and would like to thank you for giving me the training and experience which have made such a promotion possible.

Yours sincerely

Simon Jones

HOME AND FAMILY MATTERS

Letters in this section cover a wide variety of topics — schools, repairs to household items, goods bought, complaints, house purchases, etc. Because of the diversity of the subject matter, perhaps the best advice for the letter writer is to remember to reach the point of your letter quickly, giving all the facts that you feel are relevant to the subject of the letter.

The style and tone of your letter will depend very much not only on the subject matter, but also upon your relationship with the recipient. Remember that a constructive but firm line will usually work better than a blustering or abusive tone, even when the letter is one of exasperated complaint.

Letter requesting service to central heating

4 Apley Way
Borderton
Lincs
LP4 4DL

16th September 19 -

Lincoln Gas
4 Dover Street
Lincoln
LP4 6DG

Dear Sirs

We would like to have our central heating system serviced under the special 'parts only' plan advertised in the *Lincoln Post.* Our system is a Drayton 660.

There will be someone at home, each afternoon, after 2 pm.

Yours faithfully

A Barkworth

Similar letters can be used to request service to washing machines, televisions, etc. Stating the model number of the appliance in question can often mean quicker service.

Letter to hotel/guest house booking accommodation

97 Hamfirth Road
Gosholt
Avon
LXX 1PJ

16th March 19 -

The Manager
Sea View Hotel
The Promenade
Wadley Sands
Somerset
SM3 1T

Dear Sir

Further to our telephone booking of 15th March, this is to confirm that we would like a double room with sea view for six nights, arriving on 14th June and departing 20th June. We shall require full board.

I enclose a cheque for £20 deposit.

Yours faithfully

S M Parker

Letter excusing homework not done (child to give to teacher)

4 Park Road
Westleigh
Berryford
Sussex
SN3 0AD

8th November 19 -

Mr S Peterson
Berryford County Secondary School
West Meade
Berryford
Sussex
SN3 4PD

Dear Mr Peterson

Juliet was unable to complete any homework last night owing to the fact that she received rather a shining black eye playing lacross yesterday! Although the swelling has gone down considerably today, she found it very painful trying to read or concentrate yesterday evening.

I hope she keeps her head down when next playing lacross!

Yours sincerely

Elizabeth Cooper (Mrs)

Letter excusing games

4 Park Road
Westleigh
Berryford
Sussex
SN3 0AD

16th May 19 -

Miss R Simpson
Games Mistress
Berryford County Secondary School
West Meade
Berryford
Sussex
SN3 4PD

Dear Miss Simpson

I am writing to ask you to excuse Juliet from swimming for the next few weeks.

She is suffering from a very nasty inner ear infection at the moment, and the doctor has told her she must not swim again until she has visited his surgery on 28th May to check that it has cleared up. Knowing what a keen swimmer she is, I would be grateful if you could make sure she doesn't sneak into the pool before that time.

Yours sincerely

Elizabeth Cooper (Mrs)

Letter putting child's name down for preparatory school

Old Farm
Mapleford
Hants
SO4 3AX

7th July 19 -

Dr W R Weston
Headmaster's House
Shipley Court Preparatory School
Fawley Lane
Long Melford
Suffolk
GU12 4ST

Dear Dr Weston

Our son Mark was born on the 28th June, and I am wasting no time in asking you to consider him as a boarding pupil for Shipley Court.

As you know, I was a pupil there myself, as was my father before me. I cannot think of a better preparation for life than that which is provided at Shipley Court, and it would give my wife and myself enormous satisfaction to think that our son was to receive such fine educational and sporting opportunities.

We would prefer Mark to begin in the winter term following his 9th birthday and, of course, I should like him to join Askins, my old house.

My best wishes to Mrs Weston.

Yours sincerely

Peter M Hayward

Letter asking for place in a primary school

14 Fairfax Drive
Willerton
Cheshire
LP4 1SJ

16 June 19 -

The Headmaster
St Peter's Primary School
School Lane
Hartley
Cheshire
LP4 0BN

Dear Sir

We would like our son, Thomas, to enrol as a pupil at St Peter's at the beginning of the next school year, when he will be five years old. Thomas is a bright boy, with what seems to be an almost endless desire to learn.

Yours faithfully

John Sudbury

Use similar letters for requests for places in secondary or nursery schools.

Letter removing child from school because of moving

16 Shortcroft Road
Grazeley
Middlesex
TW14 35X

28th January 19 -

Miss M Metcalfe
Headmistress
Hampton Park County Secondary School
Grazeley
Middlesex
TW14 3RR

Dear Miss Metcalfe

I am writing to inform you that our daughter, Rachel, will be leaving Hampton Park at the end of this present term.

My husband's business has necessitated a move to Newbury, Berkshire, and Rachel will be attending Middle Hill School, a school just outside Newbury with, I understand, an excellent academic record.

Thank you for all the encouragement that you and your staff have given to Rachel during the last two years.

Yours sincerely

Ester Walters (Mrs)

Letter requesting absence of child from school

4 Park Road
Westleigh
Berryford
Sussex
SN3 0AD

4th November 19 -

Miss S Butcher
Headmistress
Berryford County Secondary School
West Meade
Berryford
Sussex
SN3 4PD

Dear Miss Butcher

Do you think it would be possible for Juliet to be excused from school on the 15th November? She has won a nature competition in a magazine, and her prize is a visit to an RSPB reserve. The 15th November has been chosen by the RSPB, since some interesting work is being carried out on that day.

I'm sure Juliet would be happy to tell her class of her experience, and of course the visit is in itself educational.

Yours sincerely

Elizabeth Cooper (Mrs)

Letter excusing religious instruction

18 Victoria Road
Berryford
Sussex
SN3 1SO

Miss S Butcher
Headmistress
Berryford County Secondary School
West Meade
Berryford
Sussex
SN3 4PD

14th August 19 -

Dear Miss Butcher

Our son Sikandar is to be a pupil at your school at the start of the winter term, and I am taking this opportunity to request that he be excused from religious instruction.

Although he was born in this country he has been raised in the Sikh faith, and receives instruction according to our own religion.

Yours sincerely

Dilip Patel

Letter removing child from unsuitable school

33 Silverthorne Way
Ringmead
Oakleigh
Berkshire
SL4 1BJ

23rd January 19 -

Mr W Richardson
Headmaster
Brookfield School
Borsfield
Berkshire
SL4 0AK

Dear Mr Richardson

I am writing to inform you that our daughter, Carol, will be leaving Brookfield School at the end of next term.

Although she has only been at Brookfield one term, it was always our hope that she would attend St Mary's School here in Oakleigh, since music is her great love, and is a subject greatly encouraged at that school. A place has now been made available.

I would like to say, however, that Carol has found Brookfield School an enjoyable place to study — even for so short a time — and has made many friends.

Yours sincerely

Simon Williams

Letter to school requesting appointment to inspect

3 The Close
South Park
Brockhurst
Glos
7HP 1X

15th May 19 -

The Headmaster
Shipley Court Preparatory School
Fawley Lane
Long Melford
Suffolk
GU12 4ST

Dear Sir

Would it be possible for my wife, myself and our son James to visit Shipley Court during September?

Rather belatedly, I am afraid, we have decided we would like James to attend a preparatory boarding school, and a good friend of ours, Simon Wilkinson, has recommended your school highly. Simon's own two sons are, of course, at Shipley Court, and are very happy there, as well as benefiting from the excellent facilities offered.

If September is convenient, perhaps you would be good enough to indicate a suitable date. Should September be impractical, please suggest a date in an alternative month.

Yours sincerely

Richard Smith-Heston

Letter explaining child's problem caused by teachers

17 Wexford Road
Bayford
Essex
EP4 0AN

16th February 19 -

Mr P Bowlson
Headmaster
Highfield Primary School
Dean Road
Bayford
Essex
EP4 1SD

Dear Mr Bowlson

Our daughter Anne seems to be experiencing a problem with one of her teachers, Mrs Woolacot.

I understand Mrs Woolacot takes Anne for science, and this has always been her weak subject. As you probably know she is very keen on most other subjects, but she does struggle at science, despite our coaxing at home.

I'm sure that Mrs Woolacot does not mean to pick on Anne, but because she is so much brighter at non-science subjects Anne might give the mistaken impression that she is being lazy or disinterested when it comes to science.

My wife and myself would like very much to visit your school and discuss this problem with Mrs Woolacot and yourself, in the hope that we can explain the situation, and discuss ways of assisting Anne further at home if necessary.

Both my wife and myself are free to visit the school any evening after 6 pm, except Fridays.

Yours sincerely

Michael Dewhurst

Letter excusing absence of child from school

4 Park Road
Westleigh
Berryford
Sussex
SN3 0AD

4th November 19 -

Miss S Butcher
Headmistress
Berryford County Secondary School
West Meade
Berryford
Sussex
SN3 4PD

Dear Miss Butcher

Juliet has been unable to attend school for the last two days due to a severe bout of flu. She came down with it on Saturday evening, and although she is now feeling much better, the doctor has told us she must not return to school until Friday.

Yours sincerely

Elizabeth Cooper (Mrs)

Letter explaining child's problem caused by bullying

24 Whitfield Avenue
Bayford
Essex
EP4 3PN

12th March 19 -

Mr P Bowlson
Headmaster
Highfield Primary School
Dean Road
Bayford
Essex
EP4 1SD

Dear Mr Bowlson

Our daughter Susan came home in tears last night. Apparently she has been the victim of a group of older girls who pick on the most junior pupils and demand money from them. When my daughter refused to hand over the little money she had with her, she was punched and kicked by several of these older girls.

Susan does not tell tales, and can normally look after herself, but this seems to be a particularly nasty form of bullying. She does not know the names of all the girls involved except one, Karen Wilcox, who appears to be the ringleader.

As today is Friday, I am keeping Susan at home for the weekend. She is still very upset, and quite badly bruised. I intend to telephone you on Monday morning, when you will have received this letter, to seek assurances from you that this bullying will be nipped in the bud, and the culprits punished.

Yours sincerely

Carol Potter (Mrs)

Letter to purchaser regarding sale of house

32 Church Gardens
Dunham
Bucks
SBB 3DX

4th July 19 -

Mr and Mrs S Boyer
16 Berry Close
Dunham
Bucks
SBB 5SN

Dear Mr and Mrs Boyer

<u>32 Church Gardens</u>

I understand from our solicitors that all the arrangements both for the sale of the above property, and for our purchase of New Farm, are proceeding satisfactorily, and that exchange of contracts should take place at the beginning of August. Completion should then take place at the end of the third week in August.

As agreed, I am listing hereunder items that we are selling as 'fixtures and fittings', but which do not form part of the main contract.

Brass door handles throughout;
Carpets and underlays in all downstairs
rooms and hall, landing and stairs;
lounge wall lights; roller blinds in kitchen
and bathroom; curtains in master
bedroom £550.00

Please make out a cheque in this sum payable to R. & J. Austin,
and send it to our solicitors prior to completion.

Yours sincerely

Robin Austin

Letter to estate agent regarding sale of house

32 Church Gardens
Dunham
Bucks
SBB 3DX

19th May 19 -

Miss M Wicks
Messrs Robinson Whitlow
19-21 High Street
Dunham
Bucks
SBN 13D

Dear Miss Wicks

<u>32 Church Gardens, Dunham, Bucks</u>

This is to confirm our agreement that your company will act as
sole agents for the purchase of the above property at a
commission rate of $1\frac{1}{2}$% plus VAT. We understand that should
we at any time decide to offer the house for sale through joint
agency, then the commission rate due to your company will be 2%
plus VAT assuming your company introduces an eventual
purchaser.

We further confirm that the sales particulars you have supplied
are satisfactory.

Yours sincerely

Robin Austin

Letter to solicitor regarding sale of house

32 Church Gardens
Dunham
Bucks
SBB 3DX

16th May 19 -

Messrs Upley, Pope and Dykes
5-7 Broad Street
Dunham
Bucks
3SB 1BN

Dear Sirs

<u>32 Church Gardens, Dunham, Bucks</u>

This is to confirm our conversation of 14th May with Mrs Williams of your office, whereby we agreed to your company handling the conveyancing arrangements both for the sale of 32 Church Gardens, Dunham, Bucks, and the purchase of New Farm, Chilton Matravers, Bucks. Your estimated fee was £750.00 plus VAT, stamp duty, land registration, searches and mortage costs.

The purchasers of 32 Church Gardens are:

> Mr & Mrs S Boyer
> 16 Berry Close
> Dunham
> Bucks
> SBB 5SN

The vendors of New Farm are:

> Mr & Mrs R Chapman

Please let me know what further information you require in the form of mortgage account numbers, deeds, etc.

Yours faithfully

Robin Austin

Letter to builder requesting an estimate

38 Ellerton Drive
Copley
Lancs
LNP 4DJ

Copley 61544

16th September 19 -

Messrs Stokeley & Wicks
  (Builders) Ltd
46 Winlow Lane
Brackley
Lancs
LNP 1ST

Dear Sirs

Would you please come and give us a written estimate for some alterations we wish to have carried out.

Basically the work entails removing an adjoining wall between two rooms, sealing up one doorway, and altering the position of one of the radiators and the light switch.

We would like to have this work carried out within the next three months. Please telephone us at any time to arrange a visit.

Yours faithfully

George Wills

If you do not have headed note-paper, do not forget to include your telephone number where a supplier or business may wish to contact you by this method.

Letter to builder accepting an estimate

38 Ellerton Drive
Copley
Lancs
LNP 4DJ

13th October 19 -

Messrs Stokely & Wicks
  (Builders) Ltd
46 Winlow Lane
Brackley
Lancs
LNP 1ST

Your ref SW 63/GW

Dear Sirs

This letter is to confirm our acceptance of your estimate dated 4th October, 19 -.

We also confirm that a commencing date of 3rd November is satisfactory.

We look forward to seeing you then.

Yours faithfully

George Wills

Letter to builder refusing an estimate

38 Ellerton Drive
Copley
Lancs
LNP 4DJ

13th October 19 -

Messrs Stokeley & Wicks
  (Builders) Ltd
46 Winlow Lane
Brackley
Lancs
LNP 1ST

Your ref SW 63/GW

Dear Sirs

We are in receipt of your estimate dated 4th October 19 - .

I am sorry to have to tell you, however, that the figure quoted is in excess of others that we have received, and we shall therefore not be pursuing the matter further with you.

Thank you for supplying your quotation, nevertheless.

Yours faithfully

George Wills

Letter to builder complaining about work carried out

38 Ellerton Drive
Copley
Lancs
LNP 4DJ

15th December 19 -

Messrs Stokeley & Wicks   Your ref SW 63/aw
  (Builders) Ltd
46 Winlow Lane
Brackley
Lancs
LNP 1ST

Dear Sirs

You recently carried out some structural alterations and redecoration at our house, but I have to tell you that the work has proved to be most unsatisfactory.

Although initially all seemed to be fine, large cracks have appeared throughout the new plasterwork on the ceiling. Furthermore, moving the radiator has resulted in a constant leakage from the union with the pipework. No amount of tightening seems to cure this.

I would be grateful if you would come and rectify these problems as soon as possible since, apart from the unsightliness of the ceiling, it is impossible to use the radiator at present.

Yours faithfully

George Wills

Letter complaining to neighbour about smoke

84 Brownlow Gardens
Easterley
Yorks
YK3 1P

27th July 19 -

Dear Mr Heslop

I am sorry to appear un-neighbourly, but I really must ask you to exercise a little more thought with regard to your bonfires.

Whilst understanding your necessity, like everyone else's, to burn garden rubbish, could I suggest that you refrain from doing it when the wind is blowing in a strong southerly direction. It is quite impossible to sit in the garden when you have a bonfire in such conditions, and the smoke also penetrates into the house, even with the windows closed.

Trusting that you will see that we are put to no further inconvenience.

Yours sincerely

Peter Hicks

Similar letters can be used, with slight alteration, for complaining about overhanging branches, noise, etc.

Letter complaining to neighbour about a dog

84 Brownlow Gardens
Easterley
Yorks
YK3 1P

14th Jan 19 -

Dear Mr Heslop

I am sorry to appear un-neighbourly, but I must really ask you to do something to control your dog. It has recently decided to extend its territory to include our garden, with the result that a number of plants have been spoiled, and large holes have appeared in the borders.

It seems that the problem has occurred due to your fence not being in order, allowing your dog free access.

Trusting you will see that we are put to no further inconvenience.

Yours sincerely

Peter Hicks

Letter objecting to environmental nuisance

36A Rowner's Way
Copley
Sussex
SN3 1PJ

16th May 19 -

The Environmental Health Officer
Copley Borough Council
Municipal Buildings
High Street
Copley
Sussex
SN3 4PP

Dear Sir

I wish to complain about the early start being made by builders working on the flats in Spellthorne Park Road, which is only a few metres from our back garden.

For the last few days work has commenced as early as 5 am! Since they are laying bricks, you can imagine the noise. Surely such an early start cannot be permitted, for it is almost impossible to sleep once they have begun.

I would be most grateful if you could look into this matter as soon as possible, to ensure that work begins at a more reasonable time.

Yours faithfully

S J Carter

The importance of such a letter is to bring the matter to the attention of the relevant body, who will then deal with it. The letter can be modified to cover poor roads, smells, etc. Look under the entry for Council in your telephone directory for the relevant body to contact.

Letter requesting a free sample of advertised goods

8 Birchfield Drive
Actonbury Abbas
Dorset
DN4 3DD

8th May 19 -

Castle Flooring Ltd
Dept DM 15
Queen Mary's Road
London
NW6 3KT

Dear Sirs

Please send me a free sample of your 'No waste' floor covering. I enclose a stamped, self-addressed envelope.

Yours faithfully

N Chatterton

There is no need to say in what publication you saw the advertisement. The letters and numbers in 'Dept DM 15' are the advertisers' own system of coding, telling them in what publication you read their advertisement.

Letter requesting goods advertised in a publication

8 Birchfield Drive
Actonbury Abbas
Dorset
DN4 3DD

16th Sept 19 -

Countryways Fashion Wear Ltd
Countryways House
North Temple Street
Leeds
LN6 1RR

Dear Sirs

Please send me one pair of 'Elegant Rider' fashion boots as

advertised in issue 24 of *Countryside* magazine at £19.50. I require a pair of size 5 boots, preferably in dark tan. My second choice colour is old English green.

I enclose a cheque in the sum of £21.00 to include postage and packing.

Yours faithfully

Caroline Lockwood

Letter complaining about late delivery of goods

8 Birchfield Drive
Actonbury Abbas
Dorset
DN4 3DD

28th October 19 -

Countryways Fashion Wear Ltd
Countryways House
North Temple Street
Leeds
LN6 1RR

Dear Sirs

On 16th September I sent you an order for a pair of 'Elegant Rider' fashion boots, together with a cheque for £21.00. These boots have not yet arrived and, since your advertisement states one should allow 28 days for delivery, I would be pleased if you would send my order immediately.

If there has been a delay in obtaining my size or preferred colours, it would have been a courtesy to inform me. Further, I know that my order has been received since my cheque has been cashed.

I look forward to either an explanation as to the delay, or my goods, by return of post.

Yours faithfully

Caroline Lockwood

Letter to newsagent or daily supplier

37 The Chase
Kingford
Berkshire
KT4 1JQ

2nd August 19 -

Normans (Newsagents) Ltd
2 The Parade
Kingford
Berkshire
KT4 3PQ

Dear Sir

As we shall be on holiday from 5th August, will you cancel deliveries of *The Post* until 19th August, at which date we should like the delivery resumed. We shall also require the paper on 5th August.

Yours faithfully

A McDonald

Letter complaining about faulty goods (not returned)

8 Birchfield Drive
Actonbury Abbas
Dorset
DN4 3DD

9th November 19 -

Countryways Fashion Wear Ltd
Countryways House
North Temple Street
Leeds
LN6 1RR

Dear Sirs

I recently received a pair of your 'Elegant Rider' fashion boots through mail order. However, I am afraid to say that they are faulty. Whilst one boot is perfect, the other has no stitching around the back of the heel. Since the heel support is glued and then stitched, the one on this particular boot would quickly pull away.

Shall I send the boots back to you for replacement, or do you have a local stockist to whom I may take them for replacement? If I return them to you, no doubt you will refund the cost of the postage and packing?

I look forward to your reply.

Yours faithfully

Caroline Lockwood

Letter complaining about faulty goods (returned)

1 Bracken Close
Westcott
Walchester
Hants
SO5 3DX

16th July 19 -

Graphic Toys Ltd
33-35 Eastdale Avenue
Shipton
Staffs
SH4 1X

Dear Sirs

My son was recently given a Spacewriter kit for his birthday, which I enclose. As you can see, it has a manufacturing fault in the writing board, and in its present condition is unusable.

I would be grateful for a replacement or refund (including the cost of the postage of this item back to you) as soon as possible.

Yours faithfully

D Bull

Letter stating change of address

Janet and Peter
Nayland
14 Bellsize Close
Hartley
Ripon
RRN 1TG

16th May 19 -

The Manager
Central Bank Limited
4 Market Street
Hartley
Ripon
RRN 4BG

Dear Sir

Please note that from 29th May 19 - our new address will be:

16 Willmore Gardens
Hartley
Ripon
RRN 5RG
(Telephone) Hartley 23186

Yours faithfully

Janet Nayland

It is useful to put both your names at the top of the letter if you have either a joint account, or separate accounts at the same bank.

Letter to tour operator complaining about accommodation

9 Victoria Lane
Wexley
Notts
N2 6AB

26th August 19 -

The Manager
Summer Tours Ltd
27 White Lane
Nottingham
Notts
N3 7XC

Dear Sir

Holiday no HO56; Receipt no A1032

I am writing to complain about the accommodation provided for my wife and myself from 11th to 24th August 19 -.

I booked the above holiday at your offices on 16th February. At that time, I was told that we would be accommodated in an air-conditioned room with a balcony and a private bathroom. This was confirmed in writing by Mr Jones on 20th February 19 -, along with other details about the holiday. When we arrived at the hotel on 10th August we were shown to a room lacking all these amenities. We immediately pointed out the discrepancy to your courier, Alan Smith. After investigation, he informed us that the hotel had made a mistake over the booking and very much regretted that no other room was available.

The standard of the accommodation which we were forced to accept detracted considerably from our enjoyment of the holiday. Also, your company will have paid less for this room than for one of the advertised standard.

I, therefore, expect an appropriate rebate on the sum paid. I look forward to receiving this from you in the near future.

Yours faithfully

Robert Brown

Letter asking for planning permission

8 Grey Lane
Wester
Lancs
L3 9FG

9th March 19 -

The Planning Officer
Wester Council
32-34 Brick Road
Wester
Lancs
L3 3JK

Dear Sir

I wish to extend my outhouse. I enclose drawings of the proposed alteration. I would be grateful if you would advise me on whether an application for planning permission is required for this modification.

If so, please send me the relevant form and give me an indication of the length of time it usually takes to process such an application.

Yours faithfully

Edward Cramer

Enc 3 drawings

If the proposed change is substantial, the writer need only ask for the form. The name of the officer and relevant department varies from council to council.

Letter objecting to planning permission

18 Whistler Road
Brockford
Cheshire
C8 3UG

9th June 19 -

The Planning Officer
Brockford Council
Brockford Town Hall
218-240 Cross Road
Brockford
Cheshire
C8 6FR

Dear Sir

Application for Planning Permission no 1987

I wish to object to the proposed extension for which the above application has been made.

Having viewed the plans, I am sure that this building, if constructed, would block off the light from my lower rooms and much of my back garden during the afternoon and evening.

Therefore, I request that you reject this application.

Yours faithfully

R Hancock (Ms)

Letter objecting to dangerous crossing

16 Cross Avenue
Mossley
Essex
E7 2RD

4th February 19 -

The Highways Department
Mossley Council
19-41 High Road
Mossley
Essex
E5 9SR

Dear Sir

I wish to draw your attention to the pedestrian crossing on Cross Road, about 30 metres north of Cross Avenue. In my opinion, this crossing is a hazard.

Its siting, just over the brow of a hill, means that northbound traffic has insufficient warning of the crossing. The danger is increased after dark because overhanging trees virtually obliterate the light from the Belisha beacons and surrounding lamp posts.

I drive along this stretch of road at least twice a day and have frequently witnessed narrowly averted accidents. I urge you to act promptly before a serious accident occurs.

I feel the crossing should be resited. Warning signs before the crossing would help, but I feel they would not obviate the danger. In any event, the overhanging trees should be cut back immediately.

Please let me know as soon as possible what action you propose to take.

Yours faithfully

Anne Waters (Ms)

Letter to residents association (general)

The Charnock
Residents Association
41 Oak Drive
Groveton
Cheshire
C6 7HG

18th April 19 -

To all residents of the Charnock Road area

Dear Resident

April newsletter

I am delighted to report that the Charnock Community Centre has been given a reprieve and will be able to stay open for at least another year. The alternative plans for the building have been rejected by the Council. Thanks to everyone involved!

Another problem is being resolved, but how satisfactorily remains to be seen. As you probably know, numbers 9 to 21 Oak Drive have been empty for over 5 years, and have been allowed to fall into a very dilapidated state. We have been informed by the agents that the owner intends to demolish them to make way for a block of flats. They have promised to send me a copy of the plans in time for the next meeting.

This will be held on 29th April at 7 pm in the Large Hall, Charnock Community Centre, and all residents are welcome. I hope very much to see you there.

Yours faithfully

John Harris
Secretary

Letter enquiring about improvement grants

29 Cobble Lane
Cuffley
Cumbria
C9 6TR

The Home Improvements Officer
Cuffley Council
Cuffley Town Hall
26-38 High Road
Cuffley
Cumbria
C5 3PD

16th November 19 -

Dear Sir

I wish to install a toilet and bathroom in my house. At present it has no bathroom and an outside toilet.

I own the freehold of the house, which I bought 3 years ago. The house was built in 1935 and has a rateable value of £280.

I understand that there are various home improvement grants available. I would be grateful if you would advise me on whether I may be eligible for any of these and, if so, send me the relevant application form.

Yours faithfully

Alan Stevens

Letter returning unsolicited goods

26 Horn Lane
Bearsford
Cornwall
C7 3UD

Crown Audio Co Ltd
24-30 Crewe Road
London
N7 5DS

5th May 19 -

Dear Sir

Invoice no R978

I received a cassette, an invoice and some order forms from you yesterday through the post. Since I neither ordered nor require this cassette, I have no intention of paying for it.

If you wish to recover this property you should write to me to arrange a mutually convenient time for someone from your company to pick it up within the next month.

Please note that I do not wish to receive any more unsolicited goods.

Yours faithfully

A G Jones

Letter returning mail order goods (not faulty, but unsuitable)

7 Wheeler Street
Colburn
Surrey
S9 7FD

26th May 19 -

Chrome Mail Order Co. Ltd
Chrome House
19-31 Frank Road
London
N22 6WK

Dear Sir

Order no AS536

I am returning to you the shoes (cat. no. 83, size 5) which I ordered on 8th May and received on 23rd May. Unfortunately, on closer inspection I found that they were not exactly the colour I need.

Since I am returning these goods within the period of your money-back guarantee, I look forward to receiving a cheque for £15 from you.

Yours faithfully

A J Smith (Ms)

Letter asking friend to be executor of a will

55 Shoe Lane
Curston
Wilts
W3 8FD

18th May 19 -

Dear John

Thank you again for arranging the trip to the theatre last week. As you know, Mary and I enjoyed the show very much.

In fact, it is your well known talent for arranging things which made me think of you! I am drawing up my will and would be very grateful if you would agree to execute it. I know that I could trust you to do the job well and sincerely hope that you won't be called upon to do so for a very long time! Let me know what you think.

We wondered whether you and Joan could come to dinner next Friday. Perhaps one of you could give me a ring and let me know whether you will be free.

With best wishes

Bill

Letter to request notification of birth in a newspaper

10 Rope Avenue
Whitchurch
Surrey
S8 9WV

18th July 19 -

The Herald Advertisement Department
Globe House
43-49 Ferryview
Whitchurch
Surrey
S7 3JV

Dear Sir

Birth Announcement

Please include the following announcement in the 'Births' column of the morning edition of *The Herald* on 21st July 19 -.

Brown   On 17th July, at Whitefield Hospital, London N6, to Mary (née Peters) and John, a son, Derek Andrew.

I enclose a cheque for £15.75, which I believe is the correct amount.

Yours faithfully

John Brown

Letter to trading organisation regarding goods turning out to be faulty

Compton House
6 Fern Lane
Fairford
Essex
E8 6TY

5th October 19 -

The Manager
Comfort Home Furniture
51-53 High Road
Fairford
Essex
E9 7ES

Dear Sir

Receipt no R635

I bought a sofa (Highfield, no. 87, kingfisher) from your shop on 2nd April 19 -. Although it has certainly not received more than normal wear and tear, it collapsed yesterday. It looks to me as though it is broken beyond repair.

I would be grateful if you would arrange for it to be taken away and inspected as soon as possible.

If you agree that it is irreparable, I will require either an identical replacement or a refund.

I trust that you will give this matter your urgent attention.

Yours faithfully

David Miles

BUSINESS MATTERS

Business letters are, of course, almost as diverse as business itself. However, whether you are writing a letter enquiring about promotional prospects, or placing a large order with an overseas supplier, certain points should be borne in mind.

More than in any other type of letter, business letters must appear professional. They are your advertisement, and their presentation and construction reflect your own attitudes and ability. Try to write the sort of letter you would expect to receive in similar circumstances. It is not necessary to use 'long' words or slick phrases, but it is nevertheless true that business letters sometimes seem to have almost a language of their own, and so certain words and phrases which would appear out of place should be avoided.

Business letters frequently contain enclosures — other material sent at the same time. Your letter should state that enclosures are included, and you should ensure that they are enclosed. Remember, too, that business letters often include reference numbers or letters; quoting these when requested to not only saves the recipient time, but also shows that you have read their letter correctly.

Company stationary will invariable have its own specially designed letter heading, but the recipient's name and address should normally appear on the left-hand side, even though the sender's name and address may, for instance, range across the top of the notepaper.

Letter asking for holiday

Toy Department

Mrs F Brown   23rd March 19 -
Personnel Manager
Third Floor

Dear Mrs Brown

I would like to take two weeks of my holiday entitlement from 6-19th June inclusive, and the other two weeks from 9-22nd September inclusive.

I hope that this is convenient.

Yours sincerely

Alan Jones

Letter asking for increased salary

5 Roan Avenue
Cranton
Cheshire
C5 7TY

Mr G Smith   17th February 19 -
Manager
Accounts Department
Basco Ltd
16-28 High Road
Cranton
Cheshire
C7 8HG

Dear Mr Smith

I am writing to ask whether you would consider reviewing my salary. Since my promotion two years ago, I have received no increase. Also, over the past few months, I have taken on additional responsibility. While I welcome this, I feel that it should be reflected in my remuneration.

I would be grateful for the opportunity to discuss this matter with you.

Yours sincerely

Barry Potter

If the letter is to be sent through an internal company post, you will only need to put your address within the company, e.g. Department Al. Similarly, the addressee's name, position and department will be sufficient.

If you do not wish the letter to be seen by anyone other than the addressee, put 'Private' or 'Personal' in the top lefthand corner of the envelope.

Letter of apology for unforeseen absence

Flat 12
Broom House
19 -27 Green Avenue
Leeds
LE3 8CV

Mr G Smith
Production Supervisor
Jay Electronics Co. Ltd
28-34 Rompton Road
Leeds
LE6 4VB

5th September 19 -

Dear Mr Smith

I regret that I was unable to return to work on 4th September. I will report for work tomorrow at the normal time.

Unfortunately, my flight from Majorca (flight no. BS1084), which was due to depart at 1pm on 3rd September, was delayed by adverse weather conditions. It eventually took off at 10 am today and I arrived home at about 5 pm.

I am sorry for any inconvenience my absence may have caused.

Yours sincerely

Brian Jones

Letter asking for unpaid leave (compassionate)

4 Farren Road
London
SE6 8UH

Mr Nichols
Sales Manager
Grant & Sons Ltd
19 Church Lane
London
SE4 9IG

2nd July 19 -

Dear Mr Nichols

I would be grateful to receive your permission for me to be absent from work next week (8-12th July).

I am needed to look after my mother, who is an invalid, during this week. The person who normally looks after her is required urgently elsewhere next week. At such short notice, I have been unable to arrange alternative care. This is an exceptional situation, which I do not anticipate recurring.

I hope that you will give my request sympathetic consideration. I appreciate that I would not be paid for this week.

Yours sincerely

Jane Ryman

If granted paid compassionate leave, omit the last sentence.

Letter asking for unpaid leave (other)

7 Hoar Lane
Leightown
Cornwall
CO9 4DE

Mr R Buick   20th October 19 -
Financial Director
Croftdown Ltd
Leightown
Cornwall
CO3 1AS

Dear Mr Buick

I am writing to ask you to allow me to take one week's unpaid leave from 15-22nd November.

Greyfriars College has written to ask me whether I would like to take advantage of a vacancy on one of their courses, produced by a cancellation. I have been trying to get on this course for over two years. Places are so sought-after that, if I turn down this opportunity, it might be several years before I get another chance. Unfortunately, since I could not foresee this unexpected offer, I have already used up my holiday entitlement for this year.

I do not have any pressing work engagements during this period. I hope, therefore, that you will find it possible to grant this request.

Yours sincerely

Jane Brown

Letter asking for transfer to different department

Laboratory B5

Mr H Green   3rd April 19 -
Personnel Manager
Block H

Dear Mr Green

I am writing to request a transfer to laboratory B1. There are two principal reasons for this request.

Firstly, I am particularly interested in some of the problems which this laboratory plans to initiate research on.

Secondly, a personality clash has arisen over the past few months, which I find very disturbing. I have, otherwise, been very happy during my three years of employment here.

I feel that my knowledge and experience would be equally well suited to the work in laboratory B1. The project I have been working on for the past year should be completed in a month and it would create the minimum disturbance if I transferred then.

I hope that you will give this matter your favourable consideration.

Yours sincerely

Jane White

Letter offering resignation

4 Oak Road
Creigh
Notts
NO7 3SD

Mr D Hobbis   29th September 19 -
Sales Manager
Creen & Sons Ltd
25 Weldon Road
Leeds
LE1 8NM

Dear Mr Hobbis

I have been offered, and have decided to accept, the position of Sales Manager with Broom & Sons Ltd. I am writing, therefore, to

112

give you the appropriate four weeks notice to terminate my employment with the Company on 27th October.

I have been very happy during my five years here and it was with some sorrow that I reached this decision. However, my new position offers considerably more scope and responsibility than my present one.

I would like to take this opportunity to thank you for all the support and guidance you have given me over the past five years.

Yours sincerely

Frank Rane

If you have not been happy in your employment, you may want to omit the last two paragraphs.

Letter accepting resignation

Creen & Sons Ltd
25 Weldon Road
Leeds
LE1 8NM

Mr F Rane   1st October 19 -
4 Oak Road
Creigh
Notts
NO7 3SD

Dear Frank

Thank you for your letter of 29th September resigning your employment with the Company on 27th October, which I accept with reluctance.

Your new position seems to be an excellent opportunity, which you richly deserve. I am only sorry that the Company cannot offer you anything comparable at the present time.

I am grateful for the initiative and enthusiasm which you have brought to your job over the past five years and wish you every success in the future.

Yours sincerely

David Hobbis

Letter enquiring about prospects

16 Frome Road
Sampter
Essex
ES3 8UJ

17th May 19 -

Mr H Jones
Personnel Manager
Hampton & Co. Ltd
19-27 High Road
Sampter
Essex
ES7 4ED

Dear Mr Jones

I have been working in the Sales Department for five years.
During this time the Company has trained me in many aspects of
general office procedure, computer programming and finance.

My present job of Stock Controller does not stretch me, however,
and gives me little opportunity to make use of this training.

I would, therefore, welcome the opportunity to extend the scope
and variety of my work and would be grateful for your advice on
the prospects for this here or in a sister company.

Yours sincerely

Gerald Simpson

Letter of complaint about washing facilities

Accounts Department
Third floor

Ms D Kenny   6th February 19 -
Personnel Manager
Fifth floor

Dear Ms Kenny

I wish to draw your attention to the washing facilities on the third
floor. Only one sink is provided for over one hundred male
employees on this floor. There is usually neither soap nor clean
towels available.

This must be detrimental to the health of employees and is certainly a waste of the Company's money since much work time is lost in queuing for the use of these inadequate facilities.

I would be grateful if you would look into this matter urgently, with a view to providing adequate, well-maintained facilities.

Yours sincerely

On behalf of the Accounts Department
John Harris

Letter asking for promotion

2 Hornsby Terrace
Upton
Surrey
SU8 3WE

Ms K Tope
Accounts Manager
Smith & Co. Ltd
54-58 Pine Road
Upton
Surrey
SU4 5RF

5th June 19 -

Dear Ms Tope

I am writing to ask whether you would consider promoting me to the position of Senior Clerk.

As you know, I have been working for the Company for four years, one year as Junior Clerk and three years as Clerk.

I have undertaken the work of Senior Clerk during periods of holiday and sickness and, apart from finding the work very interesting, I believe that I have performed it satisfactorily.

I have a number of ideas for improving the efficiency of the Department which the scope of my present job does not allow me to implement.

I would be grateful for the opportunity to discuss this matter.

Yours sincerely

Robert Smith

Letter of complaint about canteen food

21 Hall Road
Mossley
Dorset
DO9 6TR

15th May 19 -

Mr T Smith
Personnel Manager
Crofts Ltd
Mossley
Dorset
DO7 4DF

Dear Mr Smith

I wish to draw to your attention the reduction in the standard of food provided by the Company's canteen.

I very much appreciated the well-prepared food which used to be available in the canteen. However, in the middle of March the choice of dishes was cut from four to two, and there was a marked deterioration in quality. I have tried the canteen periodically since then and have always been served overcooked, luke-warm food. The sharp decline in the number of staff using the canteen suggests to me that my criticisms are generally held.

I would be grateful if you could explain to me why this decline in standard has occurred, and whether the Company intends to take steps to rectify the situation.

Yours sincerely

Colin Rose

Letter complaining about service

21 Plum Road
London
SW3 8YT

14th August 19 -

The Manager
Horns Ltd
23-37 Fairbridge Road
London
EC1 3SD

Dear Sir

Invoice no B512

I am writing to complain about the standard of servicing offered by your Company, and about the above invoice.

I notified your Service Department on 20th June in writing that my washing machine needed repairing. Your service engineers have since been four times — on 11th July, 18th July, 26th July and 6th August. The fault was diagnosed on the first visit and the wrong replacement part was brought by different engineers on the two subsequent visits. The correct part was fitted by the original engineer on the fourth visit.

In summary, my complaints are:
1   I had to wait three weeks for an engineer to call and nearly two months for the machine to be repaired;
2   the engineers who called on 18th and 26th July had been given inadequate or wrong information by the Company, which resulted in my taking two half days off work unnecessarily;
3   the first and fourth visits lasted a total of 30 minutes. In the above invoice, I have been charged 4 hours labour for four visits. I do not intend to pay your Company for their mistakes. Indeed, I feel it would be more appropriate if the Company offered to compensate me for the day's pay I lost through their mistake.

Therefore, I will not be paying the above invoice and look forward to receiving your response to these criticisms..

Yours faithfully

Robert Wallis

Letter of warning from employer (unofficial)

Sales and Marketing
Limited
Langdon House
Ship Street
Reading
Berkshire
DT6 8UH

16th August 19 -

Mr Brian Coulsden
12 Tree Drive
Oakley
Reading
Berks
LY9 7UN

Dear Mr Coulsden,

I am afraid that I must write to you concerning your persistent late arrival at this office. It has not gone unnoticed, and if it continues I shall be forced to take the matter to higher authority.

If you have any problem which has a bearing on this matter, please do not hesitate to come and talk to me about it. I am sure we would both prefer a solution that did not involve disciplinary action.

Yours sincerely
Sales and Marketing Limited

Peter Garton
Personnel Manager

Letter of reply to warning letter

12 Tree Drive
Oakley
Reading
Berks
LY9 7UN

18th August 19 -

P Garton Esq
Personnel Manager
Sales and Marketing Limited
Langdon House
Ship Street
Reading
Berks
DT6 8UH

Dear Mr Garton

In reply to your letter of 16th August, first of all may I apologise for causing you to have to write to me on such a matter.

My wife is in hospital at present, undergoing a major operation, and I have therefore had to get our two children ready for school before leaving for work. I have now spoken to a neighbour who has most kindly agreed to come in on three mornings a week to help us. Unfortunately she is not available on Thursdays or Fridays, and I would be grateful for your understanding on these days. I will try to make up the work at lunch times, but I am afraid that in the circumstances it is hard for me to stay late in the evenings.

I realise now that I should have explained the situation to you earlier, and hope that you will accept my apologies.

Yours sincerely

Brian Coulsden

Letter confirming an appointment

Boot Mather and Smith
12 City Chambers
London
EC3 9ZX

19th August 19 -

T Bright Esq
15 Lea Road
Dalston
Surrey
PK8 5RG

Our ref BB/TB/82

Your ref

Dear Mr Bright

Thank you for your letter of 17th August concerning the matter of your will.

I will be most happy to discuss it with you, and will expect you at 3.00 pm on Thursday 25th August.

Yours sincerely

Brian Boot

Letter making an appointment (general)

15 Lea Road
Dalston
Surrey
PK8 5RG

17th August 19 -

J Boot Esq
Boot Mather and Smith
12 City Chambers
London
EC3 9ZX

Dear Mr Boot

I would like to make an appointment to discuss my will with you. Would the afternoon of Thursday 25th, or Friday 26th August, be convenient? I am most anxious to settle matters as quickly as possible.

Yours sincerely

Timothy Bright

Letter cancelling/postponing an appointment

15 Lea Raod
Dalston
Surrey
PK8 5RG

23rd August 19 -

B Boot Esq   Your ref BB/TB/82
Boot Mather and Smith
12 City Chambers
London
EC3 9ZX

Dear Mr Boot

I am very sorry to say that I shall not be able to keep our appointment on Thursday 25th August. An urgent family matter has arisen which means that I must be out of London until at least the end of the week.

I will telephone your secretary as soon as I return, to make an alternative arrangement.

I apologise for any inconvenience caused.

Yours sincerely

Timothy Bright

Letter asking for season ticket loan

Oaklands
Lock Avenue
Broughton
Sussex
LU8 6TS

14th July 19 -

J Smith Esq
Financial Director
Mace and Pole Limited
Tower Lane
London
EC4 8JT

Dear Mr Smith

As you know, my journey into work is rather long and since the latest fares increase it is more expensive than ever. Considerable savings can be made by purchasing an annual season ticket, and I wondered whether it would be possible for Mace and Pole to advance me the money to purchase one. The repayments could perhaps be deducted from my salary each month.

I would be most grateful if such an arrangement could be made.

Yours sincerely

Michael Firth

Letter to supplier requesting details of goods/services

25 Samson Lane
Salhouse
Yorks
SL8 5RF

1st October 19 -

Champion Gates Limited
Furlong Road
Salhouse
Yorks
RT7 6YN

Dear Sir

I have seen your advertisement in *Gardening Weekly,* and I would

e grateful for some further details about your wrought iron gates,
s hereunder:

Can you supply double gates to fit an opening 2.3 metres
wide?
. What type of gate posts do you recommend?
. Can the gates be delivered, and if so at what charge?
. Could you send me a brochure showing the styles you have
available?

look forward to your reply.
ours faithfully

homas Crane

Letter from supplier requesting references or remittance

> Marston Metal
> Supplies
> Long Lane
> Marston
> Northants
> LB7 9IN
>
> 4th July 19 -

Jones Esq   Our ref JPQ/7/82
Managing Director
Maxi Components Limited   Your ref PJ/M/69
Lechford
Bucks
SL8 9IV

Dear Mr Jones

Thank you for your order of 28th June, which is receiving our
prompt attention.

Since this is the first occasion on which you have placed an order
with us, we would be grateful if you could furnish us with your
banker's or a trade reference. Alternatively we would be happy to
receive your remittance before despatch of your order.

Yours sincerely
Marston Metal Supplies

Annette Wood

Letter apologising for inability to supply goods/services

Marston Metal
Supplies
Long Lane
Marston
Northants
LB7 9IN

4th July 19 -

P Jones Esq
Managing Director
Maxi Components Limited
Lechford
Bucks
SL8 9IV

Our ref JPQ/7/82

Your ref PJ/M/69

Dear Sir

Thank you for your order of 28th June. Unfortunately we are no longer able to supply the black anodised aluminium you require, due to the introduction of new government safety regulations concerning the use of chemicals involved in the anodising process. May I refer you, however, to National Metallic Limited, Southfields Way, Broton, Yorks NW2 7DX, who import a similar product which does not infringe the Government safety regulations.

I apologise for this inconvenience, and hope that we may continue to supply your other aluminium requirements.

Yours faithfully
Marston Metal Supplies

Annette Wood

When writing letters in the course of your business, it is particularly important to put all the relevant information clearly and concisely, and to be polite at all times. State your appreciation of any order or letter to which you are replying, with its date. Set your requirements or answers out clearly, but avoid phrases such as 'thank you in advance', which preclude a refusal on the part of your correspondent. State your willingness to provide any further information needed, or your hope to be of further service to a customer.

Letter apologising for delay in supplying goods/services

Marston Metal
Supplies
Long Lane
Marston
Northants
LB7 9IN

Jones Esq
Managing Director
Maxi Components Limited
echford
Bucks
L8 9IV

4th July 19 -

Our ref JPQ/7/82

Your ref PJ/M/69

Dear Mr Jones

Thank you for your order of 28th June. Unfortunately deliveries have been delayed slightly due to the rail strike, but your bolts will be dispatched to you as soon as possible. If you have not received them within two weeks, we would be grateful if you could notify us so that we can make alternative arrangements.

We appreciate your co-operation.

Yours sincerely
Marston Metal Supplies

Annette Wood

Letter from a business apologising for a mistake

Corbett and Penn
Limited
Orbit House
Longway
Bucks
HY6 8UG

Smith Esq
Crown Paper Supplies
Fieldhouse Way
Longway
Bucks
HY7 4RF

18th May 19 -

Dear Mr Smith

I am writing to apologise most sincerely for our mistake in

supplying you with white envelopes instead of the cream ones that you ordered.

I have today despatched your correct order by special delivery, and I trust that it will have arrived by the time you receive this letter.

Please accept our regrets; I hope that we may continue to enjoy your valued custom.

Yours sincerely

Robert Adams
Managing Director

A short letter of acknowledgement

Universal Product Limited
Crown House
Marshall Street
Southware
Middlesex
YT6 4RV

16th July 19 -

D Damion Esq
Fitzroy Motors Limited
151-153 Deanly Street
London
SW1 EQ2

Our ref 982/jp

Your ref LM 21320

Dear Mr Damion

Thank you very much for your order no. 23496, dated 12th July 19 -.

The order is receiving our immediate attention and will be despatched to you by the end of this week.

I hope we may continue to receive your valued custom.

Yours sincerely

John Jones
Managing Director

Letter of query to HM Customs and Excise

Marston Metal
Supplies
Long Lane
Marston
Northants
LB7 9IN

4th July 19 -

HM Customs and Excise
VAT Office
Hope House
Corporation Street
Marston
Northants
SG8 6UO

Our ref VAT/34/82

Your ref 321 4121

Dear Sir

Relief from VAT on bad debts

I understand that provision exists for relief from the VAT lost by registered traders when a debtor becomes formally insolvent.

I would be grateful if you could send us details of how this relief can be obtained, and also whether it can be obtained in respect of debtors who became insolvent before the end of the last tax year.

Yours faithfully
Marston Metal Supplies

Michael Morris
Chief Accountant

Circular letter (mailing shot) offering goods/services

Brown's Motor
Repair Company
Brighton Road
Colbridge
Sussex
RT5 7YH

Tel 0393 76567

April 19 -

Dear

If you drive a car then we think we can help you.

With our up-to-the-minute equipment and a team of experienced motor engineers we can service your car to keep it in tip-top condition, and can carry out all engine and body work repairs.

MOT tests can be carried out while you wait, with no need to make an appointment.

If we need more than three days to repair your car we will supply you with another vehicle at highly competitive rates, and give you a full tank of petrol — FREE.

For your added convenience our engineers can come to your house and solve many of those annoying little problems without you even going outside your own front door.

So, if your car isn't quite perfect — or even if it is and you want to keep it that way — just pick up your 'phone — any of our staff will be delighted to help you.

Yours sincerely

James Brown
Managing Director

If a mailing shot is designed to look like a personal letter, take the trouble to find out the names of your potential clients, and fill in their names. Such letters should also be personally signed.

CLUBS AND SOCIETIES

Letters in this category can range from the formal to the semi-formal. If you are writing on behalf of a club or society it is usual to state, after your name, in what capacity you are acting.

Letter of application to join a club

3 Ferndale Road
Frimley
Lancs
L8 3UF

3rd May 19 -

Mr R J Ellis
The Secretary
Frimley Gardening Club
19 Bowler Lane
Frimley
Lancs
L9 4HD

Dear Mr Ellis

I wish to apply for membership of the Frimley Gardening Club.

I have been a keen gardener for many years. Mrs Brown has outlined to me the Club's activities and it sounds exactly what I need to help me be a little more adventurous!

Please send me an application form and any other information which you think may be useful to me.

Yours sincerely

John Ascot

Enc 1 stamped addressed envelope

Letter of reply to application to join a club

19 Bowler Lane
Frimley
Lancs
L9 4UD

Mr J Ascot
3 Ferndale Road
Frimley
Lancs
L8 3UF

10th May 19 -

Dear Mr Ascot

I enclose an application form, details of the subscription and this
year's Club programme. The Club year runs from January to
January and so your subscription will be seven-twelfths of that
stated if you join before the end of May.

The Club Committee considers applications for membership. Their
next meeting is on 29th June. If you return the form to me in
good time for this, I hope to be able to welcome you to our next
meeting on 6th July.

Yours sincerely

Ronald Ellis
Secretary
Frimley Gardening Club

Letter requesting club subscription

Broom Cricket Club
7 Cross Road
Broom
Oxon
O7 3OB

28th February 19 -

To all members of the Broom Cricket Club

Dear Member

Annual Subscription

The annual subscription is due by 31st March. For the year 19 - to
19 - it is £20.

You may pay me at any Club meeting or, if you prefer, send a postal order or cheque made payable to 'Broom Cricket Club' to the above address.

Please bring or send your membership card when making this payment. A record of the payment will be written in this card.

Yours sincerely

Tony Jackson
Treasurer

Letter pointing out overdue subscription (formal)

The Old Cromerian's
Football Club
12 Frimley Way
Cromer
Sussex
S6 5RF

15th April 19 -

Mr F C Brown
65 Broom Avenue
Cromer
Sussex
S7 8YR

Dear Mr Brown

Annual Subscription

According to my records, you have not yet paid your 19 - to 19 - subscription, due on 31st March 19 -.

The amount due is £20 and may be remitted by postal order or cheque made payable to 'Old Cromerian's Football Club'. I would be grateful if you would give this matter your urgent attention.

Under Club rules, failure to pay by 30th June 19 - will result in your membership lapsing automatically.

Yours sincerely

Frank Groom
Treasurer

Letter pointing out overdue subscription (informal)

The Old Cromerian's
Football Club
12 Frimley Way
Cromer
Sussex
S6 5RF

15th April 19 -

Mr F C Brown
65 Broom Avenue
Cromer
Sussex
S7 8YR

Dear Mike

<u>Annual Subscription</u>

Your subscription for this year is still outstanding. It would be a great help to me if you could clear this up quickly so that I can close the books for another year.

In case you have forgotten, the amount due is £20 and a postal order or cheque made payable to 'Old Cromerian's Football Club' will be gratefully received.

Please don't forget, because if your money doesn't arrive by 30th June your membership will cease and we will have lost our best striker!

Yours sincerely

Frank Groom
Treasurer

Letter of expulsion

Battley Cricket Club
19 Horseshoe Lane
Battley
Norfolk
NO7 5LB

15th July 19 -

Mr V Bourne
Flat 3
Gresham House
Gresham Street
Battley
Norfolk
N8 7HJ

Dear Mr Bourne

Disciplinary Hearing

Following the disciplinary hearing which you attended yesterday, the Committee met to consider what action to take.

The complaint against you was that you behaved in a rowdy and abusive manner on 15th and 22nd of May and 19th June, after Club matches.

I must inform you that the Committee decided to expel you from the Club and your membership terminates today. If you have left any possessions in the Club please let me know so that we can arrange a time for you to come and pick them up.

The Committee had to consider the detrimental effect your actions were having on the Club. For example, outings and fixtures were becoming increasingly difficult to arrange.

Your talent as a cricketer was praised by all and it was with reluctance, therefore, that the Committee reached its decision.

Yours sincerely
On behalf of the Battley Cricket Club Committee

Gary Hayes
Secretary

Letter advising formation of a society

Flat 3
Greystone Court
19-31   Greystone
Road
Chorley
Essex
E5 7YG

17th March 19 -

Mr D Green
Butler & King Ltd
6 Carriage Road
Chorley
Essex
E5 9TR

Dear Mr Green

I am writing to inform you of the formation of the Greystone Court
Tenants Association. The inaugural meeting of the the Association
was held on 12th March, at which Mr A.G. Smith (Flat 37) was
elected Chairperson, Ms F.C. Wheeler (Flat 28) Deputy
Chairperson, and I was elected Secretary.

As the landlord's agents, I am sure you will appreciate the greater
ease of communication which this allows. I would be grateful if
you would write to me on any matter concerning the Court, and I
will see that it is raised at the earliest possible opportunity.

Yours sincerely

James Stone
Secretary

Letter advising of AGM

Brougham Film Club
2 Abbey Close
Brougham
Sussex
SU8 3UD

15th March 19 -

To all members of the
Brougham Film Club

Dear Member

Annual General Meeting

This year's AGM will be held on 6th April in Conference Room H at Brougham Town Hall, 26-38 High Road, Brougham. I enclose the agenda for this meeting and the minutes of last year's AGM.

The AGM not only elects a new Committee, but also takes many decisions about the Club and its activities over the forthcoming year. I do hope, therefore, that you will be able to attend.

Yours sincerely

John Carne
Secretary

Letter requesting a motion to be put on the agenda

6 Keyne Lane
London
SE4 7GF

6th September 19 -

Mr F Brown
The Secretary
Dorling Social Club
41 Church Lane
London
SE4 8FX

Dear Mr Brown

I am submitting the following motion for inclusion on the agenda of the next Club meeting (21st September).

135

'This Club, recognising the heavy workload of the Treasurer, agrees to create the new office of Assistant Treasurer. The Club further agrees to elect an Assistant Treasurer at this meeting.'
Proposer: Alan Thomas
Seconder: Colin Reynolds

As we all know, the office of Treasurer is in danger of becoming a full-time job. I hope that this motion, if passed, will help to alleviate the situation.

Yours sincerely

Alan Thomas

Letter requesting club fixtures

20 Kings Road
London
SE4 3KL

21st January 19 -

Mr F Brown
The Secretary
Dorling Social Club
41 Church Lane
London
SE4 8FX

Dear Mr Brown

I have recently taken on a number of new commitments and I would like to ensure that they do not conflict with Club functions and meetings, which I enjoy very much.

Therefore, I would be grateful if you would send me a list of the Club's activities as far ahead as possible.

Yours sincerely

Alice Ronan (Ms)

Letter of reply to request for club fixtures

Dorling Social Club
41 Church Lane
London
SE4 8FX

28th January 19 -

Ms A Ronan
20 Kings Road
London
SE4 3KL

Dear Ms Ronan

I enclose the Club's programme for this year. More activities may be added and these will be notified to members at the monthly meetings.

I am delighted that you have enjoyed the Club's functions to date. If there are any activities missing from the list, which you would like the Club to be offering, perhaps you would inform the Committee. We rely on suggestions and comments from members in drawing up the yearly programme.

Yours sincerely

Frank Brown
Secretary

Enc 1 sheet

ILLNESS AND DEATH

These can be among the most difficult letters to write, for obvious reasons. There is no need to dwell on the illness or death which may be the subject of your letter, although your letter should, of course, express the sympathy which is intended. Letters should normally be brief and to the point. Where the illness is less serious, or where the writer of the letter is merely thanking the sender for good wishes or a gift then a lighter, even humorous, approach is quite acceptable.

Letter of condolence (informal)

3 Fairfield Way
Ousedale
Yorks
YY3 1PJ

19th September 19 -

Dearest Ruth

How very sorry I was to hear of your father's death on Friday. It must have been a particularly bitter blow, since he seemed to be getting so much better.

There is so little one can say in these circumstances, but you know that Simon and I feel the loss almost as much as you do, for he was like a second father to us as well.

I know that you are bound to be extremely busy for the next few days, but please may I come and help? I'm sure there's something I can do. I'll telephone you tomorrow, after you have received my letter.

All our love

Jane and Simon

This type of spontaneous letter has to 'come from the heart'. Don't force yourself onto another at this time unless you really mean it.

Letter of condolence (formal)

21 West Alpton
Street
Kingley
Lincs
KL4 1X

19th June 19 -

Dear Mrs Burroughs

I was deeply sorry to hear the news of Peter's sudden death last Tuesday. Please accept my sincerest condolences. I don't think I need to tell you how much he was respected and liked by everyone at the club, and he will be greatly missed.

If there is anything that I can do to help in any way, you must not hesitate to ask.

With kindest regards

George Redman

Reply to letter of condolence (formal)

3 Manor Way
Kingley
Lincs
KL4 4DL

8th July 19 -

Dear Mr Redman

Thank you very much for your kind thoughts and words. It gives me great comfort to know how highly everyone thought of Peter.

With kindest regards

Wilma Burroughs

Letter of sympathy on hearing of illness (informal)

20 Lilac Close
Borham
Dorset
D7 3ER

6th July 19 -

Dear Mary

I was very sorry to hear from John, when he got back from school, that Michael is ill. I do hope that it is not too serious and that he will be up and about again soon.

In the meantime, it would be no trouble for me to take Ruth and Anna to and from school with my own tribe and do your shopping and so on. If I can help in these or any other ways, please let me know.

John has asked me to send his best wishes to Michael.

With love from

June

Letter of sympathy on hearing of illness (formal)

Flat 1
34 Bridle Road
Leeds
L6 2KJ

15th June 19 -

Dear Mrs Brown

I was so sorry to learn of Mr Brown's accident. It must be a very trying time for you both. If there is anything that I can do to help either of you, I hope that you will not hesitate to contact me.

Please accept my sympathy and convey my best wishes for a speedy recovery to Mr Brown.

Yours truly

Jane Roberts

Letter of sympathy regarding invalid (likely to recover)

12 Lauderdale
Avenue
Frodsham
Norfolk
N9 2RE

2nd December 19 -

Dear Mr Brown

Please accept my sympathies during your wife's illness. I was relieved to hear that a diagnosis has been made and that she may well be on the road to recovery. This must have raised both your spirits considerably.

I hope to see Mrs Brown up and about again soon. In the meantime, please give her my best wishes.

Yours sincerely

Ronald Grey

Letting of sympathy regarding invalid (not likely to recover)

The Croft
51 Amble Lane
Rexford
Somerset
S3 8UH

5th March 19 -

Dear Mrs Smith

I was very sorry to hear that your husband has had to go into hospital again. It must be a very trying time, and my husband and I deeply sympathize with you both.

I know how busy you must be, but I hope you know that you are always welcome to drop in here at any time. One or both of us is usually at home.

Yours truly

Anna Davies

Letter of sympathy to invalid (likely to recover)

138 Pine Road
Brane
Herts
HE3 9IJ

23rd February 19 -

Dear Uncle Bill

Jack and I have been very worried about you — it sounded as though you were having a very tough time. I am so pleased that you are now on the mend and that the doctors expect you to make a complete recovery.

I was looking forward to seeing a bit more of you when we come up in April but, doubtless, by that time you will be back out on the golf course again!

Your loving niece

Rebecca

Letter of sympathy to invalid (not likely to recover)

18 Church lane
Sheffield
SH3 7GF

9th May 19 -

Dear Mary

I was so sorry to learn of your illness. Your mother has told us how well you have taken everything, which is just what I would have expected. Your uncle and I have always been, and continue to be, very proud of you.

I do hope that we will be able to come down and see you over the next few weeks. You are very much in my thoughts.

All my love

Aunt Ruth

Letter of thanks for sympathy on behalf of invalid

64 Oak Road
Huddleston
Devon
D4 9IJ

1st July 19 -

Dear Michael

Thank you for your letter to John, which he enjoyed very much. Although not up to writing letters yet, his condition is improving steadily and he may be out of hospital in about a month.

In answer to your question, visiting times are 2 pm to 4 pm, and 6 pm to 8 pm every day. I am sure he would be delighted to see you if you found it possible to visit the hospital.

With best wishes

Mrs Smith

Letter of thanks for sympathy by invalid

Ward 4
Greenfield Hospital
Helston Road
Surrey
S4 9NM

17th June 19 -

Dear Mr Smith

Thank you for your letter. It was so kind of you to think of me and very interesting to learn what has been going on at the Club during my absence.

I am feeling much better now and expect to be discharged sometime next week.

Please thank Mrs Smith for her good wishes which you conveyed.

Yours truly

Alan Brown

Letter of thanks for present on behalf of invalid

63 Town Road
Elford
Worcs
EL6 9RD

2nd July 19 -

Dear Freda

I would just like to thank you very much, on Mary's behalf, for the patchwork kit you sent her. It was very kind of you to remember her, and especially clever to remember that she enjoys patchwork so much. It will be a great incentive for her to recover quickly so that she can use it.

She is getting stronger by the day, and is planning a bout of 'Thank you' letters next week. I should imagine you will be top of the list!

Best wishes to George and Tony.

Carol

Letter excusing absence from work because of relative's death

2 Creek Avenue
Forsham
Lancs
LA5 9CV

23rd September 19 -

Dear Mr Smith

I regret that I was not at work today and will be unable to attend for the rest of the week. My father died suddenly yesterday evening and I am needed here to help settle his affairs and to make arrangements for the funeral. Also, the whole family, including myself, are very shaken by his death.

I expect to be back at work on Monday 29th September.

Yours sincerely

Carol Brown

Letter informing someone of a relation's death

Abbey Farm
Ludlam
Oxon
O9 6TR

15th February 19 -

Dear Mr Jones

I am very sorry to have to tell you that my brother died peacefully yesterday afternoon. Thank you for your many visits during his long illness. He was always in good spirits after seeing you.

The funeral will take place at Greenacre Crematorium, 18 Church Lane, Ludlam, at 2 pm on 19th February.

Yours sincerely

Colin Smith

Letter from employer in reply to notification of death of relative of employee

Crane Co Ltd
48 Bridge Lane
Croxford
Lancs
LA5 4PD

25th September 19 -

Ms C Brown
2 Creek Avenue
Forsham
Lancs
LA5 9CV

Dear Carol

I was very sorry to learn of your father's death. It must have been a terrible shock for you. I sympathize with you and all your family on your bereavement.

I look forward to seeing you on 29th September, if you are able to conclude your father's affairs by then.

Yours sincerely

Craig Smith

Letter for notice of death in newspaper

7 Amber Close
Kingsham
Surrey
S5 1ZM

7th April 19 -

Advertisement Department
The Kingsham Mail
26-29 Whitefield Lane
Kingsham
Surrey
S4 5QW

Dear Sir

Death Announcement

Please insert the following announcement in the 'Deaths' section
of the evening edition of *The Kingsham Mail* on 9th April. I
enclose a cheque for the appropriate amount.

> Wilson (Sarah)   On 6th April at Whitefield Hospital,
> Kingsham, much loved wife of Robert and mother of Jane
> and Susan. Funeral service at Whitefield Crematorium on
> 11th April at 10 am. No flowers please, donations, if desired,
> to Cancer Research. All enquiries to F. Dodd and Sons,
> Funeral Directors, tel: 123 4333.

Yours faithfully

Robert Wilson

Letter informing executor of death

Flat 3
Ross House
12-16 Daly Street
Whitecross
Cumbria
CU7 4DF

14th October 19 -

Dear Mr Brown

I have to inform you that my father, Bernard Smith, died yesterday
morning.

Since you are the executor of his will, I would be grateful if you would contact my mother or myself as soon as possible, so that we can discuss the settlement of his affairs.

In case my father did not tell you, his solicitors are Groom & Sons of 19 White Lane, Whitecross, Cumbria CU6 5FG.

Yours sincerely

A Jones (Ms)

Formal letter of thanks for sympathies received following death in family

Mr S G Brown and family are grateful for the very kind messages of sympathy which they have received.

9th October 19 -

64 Green Road
London
LE6 4SD

Letter to insurance company notifying of death

6 Crane Drive
Bromley
Cornwall
C7 8YT

30th June 19 -

Trust Insurance Co Ltd
69 Croft Lane
London
EC1 6DR

Dear Sir

Trust Insurance Policy no 6781

The holder of the above policy, Gerald Young, died on 28th June.

As executor of his will, I would be grateful if you would inform me of the amount of money the beneficiary will receive, and when you expect to pay this sum. Please also confirm that the beneficiary named is still Mrs G. Young.

Yours faithfully

Andrew Blake

LANDLORD AND TENANT

When there is a query or dispute between a landlord and his tenant, it is wise for both parties to put their point of view formally in a letter. If the letters are clearly written they may themselves help to clear up any misunderstandings, and an amicable solution be facilitated. If the problem is more deep seated, it is possible that legal steps may follow from one side or the other, and if this happens it will be much quicker and cheaper for everybody concerned if the points of view have been clearly stated at an early stage.

Just as for any other business letter, make sure that you acknowledge any letter you are answering, and reply to the questions it raised. State all the relevant facts and put your points firmly, but whatever your feelings may be it will never be helpful to become abusive — indeed, written abuse can lead to serious trouble.

Letter to rent officer about rent rebate

15 Albion Road
Blessop
Lancs
LR2 9PQ

15th July 19 -

The Rent Officer
Crown House
Queen Street
Blessop
Lancs
LR6 8UH

Dear Sir

I am writing to enquire about the possibility of receiving a rent rebate on my rental of the above property.

My total earnings, before tax, amount to approximately £120 per week, and no other member of my family is currently employed. Excluding rates, my weekly rent for our accommodation is £34. I have three children and am finding it hard to make ends meet, but it would be impossible for us to move to anywhere smaller since we already find our two bedrooms very cramped.

I would appreciate your advice on whether, and if so how, I may be able to get a rebate.

Yours faithfully

John Collins

Letter to Rent Tribunal about unfair rent

15 Albion Close
Blessop
Lancs
LR5 8UJ

15th July 19 -

Rent Tribunals
Crown House
Queen Street
Blessop
Lancs
LR6 8UH

Dear Sir

I am writing to ask about the possibility of getting my rent reduced.

I have been renting a two bedroomed flat at the above address for six years. We have our own kitchen and toilet, but we share the bathroom, stairs and entrance hall with another family.

My earnings amount to approximately £100 per week, before deductions, out of which I have to support two teenage sons. My rent has recently been increased by £5 to £35 per week, and this does not include any bills. In view of the poor state of repair of the house this rent seems far too high, and I would be most grateful if you could tell me how I may set about getting it reduced.

Yours faithfully

Mary Stopps (Mrs)

Letter to agent about early reoccupation

63 Oram Square
Oxridge
Oxon
6PJ 9TQ
23rd July 19 -

Mr Brian Buckland
Buckland Ballard and Partners
15 New Street
London
SW1 5PJ

Dear Brian Buckland

4 Stanswick Road

Thank you for your letter of 3rd July concerning the tenancy of 4 Stanswick Road. I would like new tenants found as soon as possible since, as you know, the financial loss involved in having an empty property is considerable.

Yours sincerely

Michael Brown

Letter to agent concerning repairs

63 Oram Square
Oxridge
Oxon
6PJ 9TQ

Mr Brian Buckland
Buckland Ballard and Partners
15 New Street
London
SW1 5PJ

23rd July 19 -

Dear Brian Buckland

Thank you for your letter of 3rd July regarding repairs to Nos 4 and 6 Stanswick Road.

Both roofs must of course be made good. Could you obtain three estimates and forward them to me for approval.

The request for a new sink unit in the kitchen of No 4 worries me a little. I see from my records that a new sink was installed only four years ago, for the same tenants. Could you visit the house and inspect the general condition in which the tenants are maintaining the property? I would appreciate your recommendation on the matter.

I shall be on holiday for four weeks from 10th August, and would like to settle all these matters before I go.

Yours sincerely

Michael Brown

Letter to Citizens' Advice Bureau about unfair eviction

24 Bourne Avenue
Blessop
Lancs
UP9 6TF

Citizens' Advice Bureau   30th August 19 -
Orion Precinct
Blessop
Lancs
UP8 6TG

Dear Sir

I would be grateful if you could tell me whether it is legal for a landlord to evict me despite the fact that I pay the rent regularly.

I have been renting a two bedroomed flat at the above address for five years, during which time I have only once been in arrears with the rent. For the past year the rent has been £25 per week and I have paid this sum to my landlord in person each week.

On 16th August my landlord told me that he needed my flat for his brother-in-law's use, and gave me notice to leave by 15th September. I have told him that I cannot find alternative accommodation and that I will not leave. Yesterday he came to say that the builders will be arriving on 6th September to redecorate the flat for his brother-in-law.

I cannot possibly find another flat and would therefore much appreciate your advice as to my legal position.

Yours faithfully

Stuart Hall

Letter from a landlord to a tenant, reminding him that the rent is due

40 Moreley Drive
Poolford
Dorset
JP8 6YB

21st May 19 -

Mr P Smith
94 Court Road
Poolford
Dorset
JO9 5TB

Dear Mr Smith

May I remind you that the rent due from you on 30th April for the property you occupy at 94 Court Road, has not yet been received.

I would be grateful for your remittance as soon as possible.

Yours sincerely

Ian Graham

Letter from landlord to tenant requesting overdue rent

40 Moreley Drive
Poolford
Dorset
JP8 6YB

3rd June 19 -

Mr P Smith
94 Court Road
Poolford
Dorset
JO9 5TB

Dear Mr Smith

I am afraid I must remind you again that the rent due on 30th April for the property you occupy at 94 Court Road, has still not been received.

Unless full payment is made within seven days of the date of this letter I shall be forced to put the matter in the hands of my solicitor.

Yours sincerely

Ian Graham

Letter of reply to landlord requesting overdue rent

94 Court Road
Poolford
Dorset
JO9 5TB

12th May 19 -

I Graham Esq
40 Moreley Drive
Poolford
Dorset
JP8 6YB

Dear Mr Graham

I am very sorry that you have had to write to me requesting payment of my rent, which I know is overdue.

The last three months have been very difficult for me since I was made redundant. However, I have now started work again and with a regular wage I will try to pay off my debt to you as quickly as possible. Would you agree to my paying an extra £3 per week until the backlog is cleared?

I realise now that I should have explained the situation to you sooner, and hope that you will accept my apologies.

Yours sincerely

Peter Smith

Letter from landlord serving notice to quit on a tenant

40 Moreley Drive
Poolford
Dorset
JP8 6YB

12th June 19 -

Mr P Smith
94 Court Road
Poolford
Dorset
JO9 5TB

Dear Mr Smith

Since I have not received any rent from you since 30th March for the property you occupy at 94 Court Road, I am now forced to give you formal notice to leave. In accordance with your tenancy agreement I am giving you two weeks' notice from the date of this letter.

Yours sincerely

Ian Graham

Letter to a landlord asking him to effect repairs

94 Court Road
Poolford
Dorset
JO9 5TB

25th May 19 -

I Graham Esq
40 Moreley Drive
Poolford
Dorset
JP8 6YB

Dear Mr Graham

During the last three days a large crack has developed in my dining room ceiling. Pieces of plaster have fallen off and additional hairline cracks are now appearing. I have been into the loft and can find no dampness or other obvious cause of the problem.

I should be most grateful if you would arrange for a builder to inspect the property as soon as possible since I fear that even more serious damage may occur.

Yours sincerely

Peter Smith

Letter to a landlord concerning recurring repairs

94 Court Road
Poolford
Dorset
JO9 5TB

18th May 19 -

I Graham Esq
40 Moreley Drive
Poolford
Dorset
JP8 6YB

Dear Mr Graham

I am afraid I must inform you that the window in our kitchen still cannot be opened more than five centimetres, despite the efforts of your workmen on 6th May.

I would very much appeciate it if you could arrange for a further attempt to be made to free it. As I am sure you will understand, my wife has been finding her kitchen less than fresh during the recent hot weather.

With many thanks for your attention in this matter.

Yours sincerely

Peter Smith

Letter to a landlord stronger in tone than the former

94 Court Road
Poolford
Dorset
JO9 5TB

25th May 19 -

I Graham Esq
40 Moreley Drive
Poolford
Dorset
JP8 6YB

Dear Mr Graham

Kitchen at 94 Court Road

I am afraid that I feel I must write to you again about the state of
our kitchen.

We received a visit from your building contractor, Mr Ady, on 14th
May, when he promised to bring a new sink unit within one week.
He also promised to repair the window the following day. Neither
of these things has happened.

As you know, the sink unit was cracked to the extent of being
unusable when we moved here on 1st April. The window has
been attended to once already, but clearly without success since
we are still unable to open it more than a few centimetres.

The hot weather recently has made the unventilated kitchen
extremely unpleasant for my wife and children, and my wife is
greatly inconvenienced by the lack of a sink.

I would appreciate your immediate attention to these matters.

Yours sincerely

Peter Smith

However justifiably angry you may feel, never threaten legal action or the
involvement of sanitary inspectors or the like unless you really intend to
carry out your threat.

Letter from a tenant asking for a rent reduction

94 Court Road
Poolford
Dorset
JO9 5TB

12th May 19 -

I Graham Esq
40 Moreley Drive
Poolford
Dorset
JP8 6YB

Dear Mr Graham

I am writing to ask if you will agree to reduce the rent I am paying for the above house.

As you know, I have lived here for eight years now and have always kept the property in excellent repair. You will also know that I have done many repair jobs myself rather than trouble you to call in workmen.

The latest rent increase will cause me considerable financial hardship and means that I will be paying considerably more than any of my immediate neighbours. I realise that the house is in better condition and might therefore command a higher rent on the open market, but I am bound to say that I feel it is rather unfair to penalise a tenant who looks after your property particularly well.

I hope you will look favourably on this request.

Yours sincerely

Peter Smith

Letter from a landlord refusing to reduce the rent

40 Moreley Drive
Poolford
Dorset
JP8 6YB

Mr P Smith
94 Court Road
Poolford
Dorset
JO9 5TB

16th May 19 -

Dear Mr Smith

I regret that it is impossible for me to reduce the rent of your house.

I appreciate that you have always been an excellent tenant and have undertaken various minor repairs yourself. However, the cost of the major work to your roof last year and the recent rate increases mean that I cannot consider any rent reduction.

I cannot discuss the rents paid by your neighbours beyond saying that the outgoings on each of my properties are different, and each has to be considered individually.

Yours sincerely

Ian Graham

Letter from a landlord raising the rent of tenant

40 Moreley Drive
Poolford
Dorset
JP8 6YB

12th May 19 -

Mr P Smith
94 Court Road
Poolford
Dorset
JO9 5TB

Dear Mr Smith

I am writing to give you formal notice that, as from 25th June 19 -, your rent will be increased from £40 to £43 per week.

I am forced to take this step owing to the recent increase in rates.

Yours sincerely

Ian Graham

Send a formal notification such as this by registered post, keeping the receipt, to avoid any dispute as to delivery. If there is a tenancy agreement the landlord should make sure to give the proper amount of notice of any rent increase.

Letter to a tenant refusing to do repairs

40 Moreley Drive
Poolford
Dorset
JP8 6YB

12th August 19 -

Mr P Smith
94 Court Road
Poolford
Dorset
JO9 5TB

Dear Mr Smith

Thank you for your letter of 1st August, requesting repairs to be undertaken on your stairs. I am afraid, however, that it is quite impossible for me to consider paying for any such major repairs for some time.

During the last two years most of the rent has been absorbed by the various repairs and redecoration work, and the property has become a severe drain on my own income.

While I do not wish to seem unreasonable, I am forced to refuse your request.

Yours sincerely

Ian Graham

Letter from a landlord to an outgoing tenant asking the latter to allow a prospective tenant to see over the house

40 Moreley Drive
Poolford
Dorset
JP8 6YB

1st October 19 -

Mr P Smith
94 Court Road
Poolford
Dorset
JO9 5TB

Dear Mr Smith

As your tenancy expires at the end of this month, may I ask if you could allow a prospective tenant to look over the house?

I would be most grateful if you would permit this. Naturally the person concerned would only come by appointment, at a time convenient to Mrs Smith and yourself.

Yours sincerely

Ian Graham

Letter from a tenant asking for an extension of time to pay the rent (1)

94 Court Road
Poolford
Dorset
JO9 5TB

16th May 19 -

Mr I Graham
40 Moreley Drive
Poolford
Dorset
JP8 6YB

Dear Mr Graham

I am extremely sorry to find that I must ask if you can possibly allow me some extra time in which to pay my rent on the above property.

I know that the rent is now overdue, but I am afraid that at the moment I am unable to find the money. The last few months have proved a great strain on my finances, largely because my wife has been in hospital and we have therefore had to manage on one income alone. On top of this my son has just started at college and this has inevitably entailed some extra expenses.

In all the circumstances could I ask you to let the matter stand for a little while and, during the interval, I will do my utmost to get the money together.

Yours sincerely

Peter Smith

Letter from a tenant asking for an extension of time to pay the rent (2)

94 Court Road
Poolford
Dorset
JO9 5TB

16th May 19 -

I Graham Esq
40 Moreley Drive
Poolford
Dorset
JP8 6YB

Dear Mr Graham

I am writing to ask whether you would be kind enough to allow me an extension of time in which to pay my rent on the above property?

I recently suffered an accident which has meant that I have been away from work for six weeks. As a result I have been very short of money. I am returning to work on Monday 20th May and will therefore soon be able to get my finances on a sound footing once more. I would be most grateful if you could agree to my paying this month's rent in two instalments at the ends of June and July.

Yours sincerely

Peter Smith

Letter from tenant who suspects defects in the house he is occupying

94 Court Road
Poolford
Dorset
JO9 5TB

30th June 19 -

Mr I Graham
40 Moreley Drive
Poolford
Dorset
JP8 6YB

Dear Mr Graham

I am writing to inform you of my disquiet at the dampness in the property I rent from you at the above address.

Throughout last winter we found it almost impossible to rid the house of its musty smell. Clothes and bedlinen were always slightly damp when taken out of cupboards or drawers; those kept in the fitted bedroom cupboard at the rear of the house being worst affected. My anxieties have increased since discovering two damp patches on the dining room wall.

I would much appreciate it if you could send a builder to assess the situation as soon as possible. It would, of course, be more pleasant for my family and more beneficial to the property if any necessary work could be carried out before the onset of another winter.

I will be most grateful for your early attention to this matter.

Yours sincerely

Peter Smith

Letter asking a landlord to release the writer from his tenancy before the lease has expired

94 Court Road
Poolford
Dorset
JO9 5TB

30th October 19 -

Mr I Graham
40 Moreley Drive
Poolford
Dorset
JP8 6YB

Dear Mr Graham

My husband has just accepted promotion to a new job near Bristol, and we are anxious to move into that area as soon as possible. I realise that our lease on this house still has three years to run, but I wonder if you would be so kind as to consider releasing us from the agreement before that time is up? If you can allow this, I would much appreciate your letting me know the date on which our tenancy could end, and the terms you would expect us to agree to.

If at all possible we would like to leave by the end of the year, and we will of course be ready to meet any reasonable terms you may offer. I am very sorry to put you to this trouble, and would like to take this opportunity of saying how much we have enjoyed living here.

Yours sincerely

Irene Smith (Mrs)

MONEY MATTERS

Letters about money matters should always be written in the clearest and most precise manner possible. It is best to avoid archaic phrases which your reader may misunderstand, and to write in concise sentences which leave no possibility of ambiguity.

When writing letters to a firm or financial institution it is best to address a particular individual. If you cannot find out the name of the appropriate person, at least make sure that your letter goes to the correct department. Within large organisations, and some smaller ones too, it can take some time for a letter to arrive on the desk of the person who can deal with it if it arrives in the post room bearing no name.

Just as with any non-personal letter, those concerning money should always be polite — even if you are angry. State the subject matter of the letter in your first paragraph, and follow through the other points you want to make in a logical order. By sticking entirely to the facts in this way, you will put your case with the least likelihood of misunderstanding or offence.

Quite often it may be helpful to enclose relevant documents such as receipts. If you do this, always send copies, not the original, and say what you have enclosed in the text of your letter. To avoid any possible difficulties at a later stage it is wisest to keep a copy of any letter you write on a financial matter.

Lastly, always quote any reference given on a letter to which you are replying. Even if you do not use references yourself they will help your correspondent and thus speed up the handling of your business.

Letter asking for a bill to be paid

Frank Acton and Company
16 Forth Avenue
London
NW16 4ER

22nd January 19 -

E Wolverton Esq
63 West Street
London
NW10 9PQ

Dear Sir

A statement of your account with this company was sent to you on 16th December. Since we have not yet received your remittance for the amount due, it is possible that our letter was mislaid in the post.

We would appreciate your informing us if this is the case, so that we can supply a copy. If you have in fact received our statement, we would be grateful for settlement of the outstanding sum.

Yours faithfully
Frank Acton and Company

John Smith
Accounts Manager

Letter pressing for a bill to paid

Frank Acton and
Company
16 Forth Avenue
London
NW16 4ER

4th February 19 -

E Wolverton Esq
63 West Street
London
NW10 9PQ

Dear Sir

We much regret having to call your attention to the account we sent to you on 16th December 19 -. Having written to you on 22nd January 19 - in case the original statement had been mislaid, we can only conclude that our requests are being wilfully ignored.

Payment is now long overdue, and we must ask that you settle the outstanding debt of £178.64 by return of post.

Yours faithfully
Frank Acton and Company

John Smith
Accounts Manager

Letter threatening proceedings for an unpaid bill

Frank Acton and
Company
16 Forth Avenue
London
NW16 4ER

6th February 19 -

E Wolverton Esq
63 West Street
London
NW10 9PQ

Dear Sir

Unless your outstanding debt to us, of £178.64, is settled within
the next seven days I shall be reluctantly forced to place the
matter in the hands of our solicitors.

Yours faithfully
Frank Acton and Company

Charles Dobson
Accounts Director

Letter requesting settlement of an account

Napley Timber
Limited
Walter's Yard
Broughton
Sussex
LU7 5TN

6th February 19 -

F Hunter Esq
63 Westerham Road
Broughton
Sussex
LU9 6TV

Dear Sir

We would much appreciate your payment for the timber supplied
to you during October and November 19 -.

We are now preparing our books for auditing and the delay in receiving your settlement is causing some inconvenience.

A duplicate statement is enclosed.

Yours faithfully
Napley Timber Limited

Brian Kent

Letter demanding settlement of an account

Napley Timber
Limited
Walter's Yard
Broughton
Sussex
LU7 5TN

15th February 19 -

F Hunter Esq
63 Westerham Road
Broughton
Sussex
LU9 6TV

Dear Sir

We regret to note that your account for timber supplied during October and November 19 - is still outstanding. We wrote to you on 6th February enclosing a duplicate statement to serve as a reminder.

In these circumstances I am afraid that unless we receive settlement within seven working days of the date of this letter, I shall be forced to instruct our solicitors to take action.

Yours faithfully
Napley Timber Limited

Peter Harvey
Managing Director

A letter threatening proceedings should never be written unless you really feel that no other course remains open and you are prepared to carry through your threat. If circumstances do demand that such a letter be sent, it is sensible to send it by recorded delivery.

Letter requesting a statement of account

14 Alloa Road
Newington
Kent
LR5 7VN

9th August 19 -

Accounts Department
Messrs Perkin and Lambton
Orbit House
Stoneley
Middlesex
ST7 4RV

Dear Sir

I should be most grateful if you would send me your statement of account up to and including 31st July 19 -.

Yours faithfully

Miles Sproggins

Letter pointing out an error in a statement

14 Alloa Road
Newington
Kent
LR5 7VN

Mr Martin Knight
Accounts Department
Messrs Perkin and Lambton
Orbit House
Stoneley
Middlesex
ST7 4RV

15th August 19 -

Your ref MS/21.8.8-

Dear Martin Knight

Thank you for sending me, as requested, your account for the three months ending 31st July 1982.

I must point out, however, that you have omitted to credit me with the value of the goods returned to you on 10th July, for which I have your receptionist's receipt.

Upon receiving a correctly amended statement I will of course send you my cheque in full settlement.

Yours sincerely

Miles Sproggins

Letter replying to a creditor

63 Westerham Road
Broughton
Sussex
LU9 6TV

P Harvey Esq   18th February 19 -
Managing Director
Napley Timber Limited
Walter's Yard
Broughton
Sussex
LU7 5TN

Dear Mr Harvey

I have this morning received your warning of legal proceedings in connection with my outstanding account. I am extremely sorry that you should feel such a step necessary, and no less sorry that I should have been the cause of it.

Since I have been a customer of yours for more than five years, and have settled my account promptly each month throughout that time, I trust that you may reconsider the matter. I have to admit that my finances have been strained recently, due to various unexpected extra costs. However, I confidently expect to return to a more solid basis next month and would be happy to issue a promissory note for the sum involved plus any reasonable interest.

I hope that you will accept this offer, and my apologies for the inconvenience I have caused.

Yours sincerely

Frank Hunter

When requesting a business favour this more personal style of letter can be successfully used. However, it should be used with caution if you do not know your correspondent personally, since it could appear presumptuous.

Letter complaining of an overcharge in an invoice

19 Baverstock Avenue
Reading
Berkshire
HY5 1SC

1st December 19 -

Accounts Department
Sportsman's Aid Limited
Sporting House
Myers Industrial Estate
Ludley
Wiltshire
YT7 4XT

Dear Sir

I have this morning received your invoice dated 25th November. As you will see, the second item is for two dozen X6 golf balls, at a total cost of £24. These were on my original order, but cancelled in writing on 15th November. I must assume that you received this cancellation, since the balls were not included in my delivery.

I am returning your invoice and when it has been amended I shall be pleased to send you my cheque.

Yours faithfully

Michael Garfield
Enc

Do not forget to enclose the invoice.

Promissory note

63 Westerham Road
Broughton
LU9 6TV

26th February 19 -

£246
Three months after date, I promise to pay Napley Timber Limited, or order, the sum of Two Hundred and Forty Six pounds sterling for value received.

Frank Hunter

170

Joint promissory note

63 Westerham Road
Broughton
Sussex
LU9 6TV

26th February 19 -

£500

Six months after date, we promise to pay Napley Timber Limited, or order, the sum of Five Hundred Pounds sterling for value received.

Frank Hunter
James Fleming

Stamp duty must be paid on promissory notes. The duty varies according to the amount of money involved.

Letter to bank confirming that a cheque should be stopped

51 Church Street
Royburn
Berkshire
6XJ 9PQ

The Manager
London and District Bank
119 Bolton Street
Royburn
Berkshire
6YN 5FV

10th July 19 -

Dear Sir

This is to confirm my telephone call of this morning asking you to stop payment of my cheque number 4248 638, dated 4th July 1982. It was for the sum of £586 and was signed by me in favour of Mr Eric Palfrey.

Mr Palfrey has not received the cheque and I must therefore assume that it has been lost in the post.

Yours faithfully

Simon Dennis

Only stop a cheque for a good reason, such as that it has been lost or that fraud is suspected.

Letter (general) confirming loss of cheque card/cheque

51 Church Street
Royburn
Berkshire
6XJ 9PQ

10th May 19 -

E R Cox Esq
The Manager
London and District Bank
119 Bolton Street
Royburn
Berkshire
6YN 5FV

Dear Mr Cox

I am writing to confirm my telephone call of this morning, in which I informed a member of your staff, Miss Jones, that I have lost my cheque card, Number 456789.

I first noticed the loss of my card this morning, and I know that it was in my wallet on 8th May when I used it to cash my cheque Number 12345 at your High Street branch.

Yours sincerely

Simon Dennis

Letter requesting credit card

51 Church Street
Royburn
Berkshire
6XJ 9PQ

6th July 19 -

The Manager
Easy Card International
International House
Deacon Street
London
W1X 5ER

Dear Sir

I wish to apply for membership of Easy Card International. As a self-employed marketing consultant it would be extremely useful to me to have the credit facilities enjoyed by Easy Card holders.

I have been running my own consultancy business for five years. My current annual turnover is £60,000, with a gross profit of £35,000. I have a business development loan from my bank, which will be paid off in May 19 -. I have no other debts of any significance.

My business and personal bank accounts are with the Bolton Street, Royburn branch of the London and District Bank. The Manager there, Mr Eric Cox, assures me that he will be glad to supply you with a reference on request.

Yours faithfully

Simon Dennis

Letter to bank advising of being temporarily overdrawn

51 Church Street
Royburn
Berkshire
6XJ 9PQ

10th March 19 -

E R Cox Esq
The Manager
London and District Bank
119 Bolton Street
Royburn
Berkshire
6YN 5FV

Dear Mr Cox

It may have come to your notice that my account (Number 5537642) has been marginally overdrawn on four occasions in the last month. With the winter fuel bills due to be paid soon, I am afraid that this will happen again, and I would be grateful if you could let me have proper overdraft facilities up to £500. I would expect to need such an arrangement until the end of July 19 -, when my salary increase should enable me to repay the debt.

I would of course be quite willing to come in and discuss the matter with you should you think it necessary.

Yours sincerely

Simon Dennis

Letter to building society advising of difficulty in paying mortgage due to redundancy

6 Amberley Villas
Burchford
Oxfordshire
LM9 6PR

1st April 19 -

Midlands Building Society
Abbey House
Upper High Road
Gloster
Oxon
LM8 9AB

Dear Sir

Mortgage policy number 898/LMR/63

I am afraid I must write to inform you that I am having considerable difficulty in meeting my mortgage repayments, and can foresee no immediate improvement in my financial situation.

My employers for the last fifteen years, J.M. Smith and Company, went into liquidation in January and I was therefore made redundant. I am of course actively seeking another position, but as you will appreciate employment is not easy to find at present in this area.

I have some savings in addition to my redundancy payment, but despite cutting back on many fronts I am finding it hard to meet all my commitments. It would cause great upset for my family if we were forced to move house, and I wondered therefore if I might be allowed to reduce my monthly payments by 20% for the present, extending the total length of my mortgage to compensate for this? After careful consideration I am certain that I could meet the interest payment regularly, and I very much hope that you will give your sympathetic consideration to my situation.

I would naturally be happy to come and discuss this matter further with you if you feel it would be helpful.

Yours faithfully

Malcolm Jones

Letter to building society advising of difficulty in mortage payment due to the death of a relative

6 Amberley Villas
Burchford
Oxon
LM9 6PR

10th December 19 -

Midlands Building Society
Abbey house
Upper High Road
Gloster
Oxon
LM8 9AB

Dear Sir

Mortgage policy number 898/LMR/63

I am sorry to inform you that my husband, Mr Malcolm Jones, in whose name the above mortgage was held, died on 6th December.

I have not yet sorted out his financial affairs, but I know that he did not have a mortgage protection policy. I believe that his life assurance policy and my widow's pension will enable me to meet the mortgage payments in the future, but I fear that I will have some difficulty in finding the funds for the next three payments or so. I wonder if it would be possible for my next three payments to be deferred and the length of the mortgage extended accordingly?

I would much appreciate your understanding at this difficult time.

Yours faithfully

Gladys Jones

Letter to hire purchase company advising of difficulty in meeting repayments

3 Seacombe Villas
Archery Fields
Arden
Kent
KJ7 6TB

6th May 19 -

Southern Credit Company
12-14 Arlington Street
London
SW1 6HL

Dear Sir

Agreement HP23/64/82

I am having some difficulty in meeting the repayments for the car that I am buying in accordance with the terms of the above agreement. The contract was signed on 12th August 19 -, and since then I have paid regularly each month. Unfortunately I now find that my commitments are more than my financial situation will stand.

I have no wish to default on my debt to your company, and would therefore much appreciate it if you would consider allowing me to make rather smaller payments over a longer period.

I would be most grateful if you could let me know whether such an arrangement is possible and, if so, what terms you are able to offer.

Yours faithfully

Peter Smithson

As with any debt about which there is some difficulty, it is advisable to write to the creditor and make whatever realistic offer you can.

Letter advising of money remitted and requesting a receipt

19 Trehurst Crescent
Buxton
Kent
MO5 2LR

6th August 19 -

Messrs Abbot and Coles
104 Smith Street
London
SE21 6AJ

Dear Sirs

I enclose a cheque for £238.56, in full settlement of your invoice Number 6583.

I would appreciate a receipt for this sum.

Yours faithfully

Ann Woods (Mrs)

Enc

Letter to credit reference agency asking for your personal file

308 Cumber Road
London
NW5 6LM

5th February 19 -

Black and Company
Credit House
Comley
Berkshire
RP6 8SJ

Dear Sir

I understand from Mr A. Mathews, the manager of Maybrick Stores, Pinder Street, London, that you are holding a file relating to my credit status. Since I have been refused credit by Maybrick Stores I must assume that the information you have about me, which you supplied to them, is unfavourable.

I would appreciate your sending me a copy of any information you have about my financial affairs, and I enclose a postal order for 25p which I understand to be the appropriate handling charge.

Yours faithfully

Andrew Blackstock

Enc

You are entitled by law to see and correct any files held on you by a credit reference agency. Any corrections must be passed on to anyone who has been given a reference on you in the last six months.

Letter to a shop asking why a request for hire purchase was refused

308 Cumber Road
London
NW5 6LM

21st January 19 -

The Manager
Maybrick Stores
108 Pinder Street
London
W1A 2AB

Dear Sir

I am writing to ask why I have been refused credit by your company.

I came to your shop on 18th January in order to buy a Hotflow 6X washing machine and a Hotflow Senior tumble drier, at a total cost of £634. Knowing from leaflets displayed within the store that you make credit facilities available to your customers I asked for the necessary paperwork to be prepared. I was most shocked when the assistant informed me that I could not have any credit, a decision confirmed by the Department Manager, Mr Smith.

I would appreciate your explanation of this refusal, which has caused me considerable inconvenience and embarrassment.

Yours faithfully

Andrew Blackstock

Under the Consumer Credit Act, traders and finance companies are not obliged to explain why they refuse to give a person credit, but they must tell you if they have used a credit reference agency provided you ask for this information, in writing, within a month of their refusing you credit.

Receipt for money

34 Chelsea Walk
Peterburgh
Lincolnshire
PB8 2GT

Received from Richard Shipman, the sum of seventy five pounds only, in payment for the Vauxhall van (registration number NYO 252J) delivered to him on 3rd April 1982.

Brian Hicks

£75   3rd April 19 -

Drafting statements and invoices

Most statements and invoices are issued by businesses who will have them printed in accordance with the legal requirements of the tax authorities. The full details of these requirements are beyond the scope of this book, and anyone wishing to issue invoices in the course of regular business should certainly seek the advice of H.M. Customs and Excise and a qualified accountant. Briefly, however, the following details should be set out clearly on any invoice or statement:

1. Your own name and address (and VAT registration number if you have one).
2. The date on which the goods or services were supplied.
3. A description which is sufficient to identify the goods or services which you have supplied.
4. The total amount payable, excluding any VAT.
5. Any cash discount.
6. The total amount of any VAT.
7. The customer's name (or trading name) and address.
8. The type of supply, such as sale, hire purchase, rental, exchange, etc.

Points 7 and 8 can be omitted by retailers selling direct to the general public. Points 4 and 6 can also be replaced by a VAT inclusive price subject to prevailing limits on the sum payable.

A statement should give your name or trading name, the date of the statement and the dates, sums and numbers of all the transactions included on it. A statement should also make clear which of the invoices on it have been paid and what total sum remains owing at the statement date.

Example of invoice

Invoice No 76
To A P Smith and Sons   14th July 19 -
48 Arbroath Road
London
NW8 6LR   Tax point 14th July 19 -

From   Motor Traders (UK) Limited
        Bowater Street
        York
        SL8 9RP   VAT Regd No 582 6543 21
Sale

Quantity	Description	Price Excluding VAT	VAT at 15%
1 2	Exhaust pipe Brackets at £10	£50 £20 £70	£ 7.50 £ 3.00 £10.50

Terms Cash discount of 5% if paid within 14 days	Total £80.50

Example of statement

AUTO MOTORS UK LIMITED   STATEMENT

Please send payment direct to Accounts Office: 58 Ebury Street
                                                 Manchester
                                                 LM8 6AT
                                                 Tel 061 898 4567

Lewis Spares
6-8 West Road
HIGH WYCOMBE
Buckinghamshire
SL7 5RQ   10th February 19 -

Date of Sale	Reference	Amount		Reference
08/01/82	42002 CSH	27.95		INV - invoice
15/01/82	42069 INV	9.82		C/N - credit
31/01/82	42098 INV	3.40		CSH - cash
05/02/82	42121 INV	16.84		received
	Balance outstanding £2.11			

Letter to insurance company advising of theft

Pigeon Cottage
Flight Hill
Banwood
Oxfordshire
SL8 5NM

21st May 19 -

Reliant Insurance Company Limited
Pimlico Street
London
SW1 6XJ

Dear Sir

Policy Number LM 169380

I am writing to report that a theft occurred at the above address
on the night of 19th May 19 -

My wife and I were both at home on the night in question, but
knew nothing of the theft until 7.30 am on the morning of 20th
May, when I realised that the kitchen window was open. We
quickly discovered that various items were missing, and
telephoned the police. I have made a full statement to the police
at Banwood Police Station, where Detective Inspector Charles is in
charge of the case.

I enclose a full list of the items that are missing, with their
replacement values. Fortunately nothing irreplaceable was taken
and I have been able to confirm the values quite easily.

I will willingly give you any further information that may be
helpful, and hope that a settlement can be made without delay.

Yours faithfully

Barry Spinks

Enc

Always inform your insurance company of any claim immediately, even if
you do not yet know the extent of the loss. Most companies will then send you
a claim form to fill in, which would take the place of the list sent with the
above sample letter.

Letter to insurance company in respect of car accident when it is your fault

60 Waldemar Avenue
London
NW16 6LR

29th June 19 -

Resteasy Insurance Company
Resteasy House
Lutton
Surrey
FT5 7YB

Dear Sir

Policy Number 685 LM 982 Z

I have to report that this afternoon, whilst driving down Maida Vale, I was involved in an accident with a car turning right into Boundary Road. Regrettably I have to admit that the collision was my fault.

My own car has suffered severe denting to the offside wing, which I believe will have to be replaced. The other car will require new head and side lights, a new front bumper and some repairs to the paintwork.

The driver of the other car (registration number RNP 852P) is Mr John Bolton of 15 Harp Gardens, London, NW3 7TX. He is insured with the Kingly Insurance Company.

I would be grateful if you could send me the necessary claims forms which I will complete and return to you as soon as I have an estimate for the repairs from my garage.

Yours faithfully

James Sudbury

Never give the go ahead for repairs to start before getting the estimate approved by your insurance company.

Letter to insurance company in respect of a car accident when it is not your fault

60 Waldemar
Avenue
London
NW6 6LR

29th June 19 -

Resteasy Insurance Company
Resteasy House
Lutton
Surrey
FT5 7YB

Dear Sir

Policy Number 685 LM 982 Z

I have to report that this evening, whilst I was driving down Maida Vale, a van overtook me and severely scraped the side of my car.

The accident was, on his own admission, entirely the fault of the other driver. His name is Ian Morton and he is an employee of Coast Deliveries (6 Oak Court, London, SE16 2XN) whose van he was driving at the time. Since no one was injured in any way, and the cause of the accident was not in dispute, the police were not called. However, a Mrs Ann Wood, of 16 Arley Road, London, N8 4SP, saw the incident clearly and has given me permission to mention her name should an independent witness be called for.

I have not yet obtained estimates for the repairs needed, but will forward them to you in the next few days.

Yours faithfully

James Sudbury

If an accident is not your fault, make certain to keep your no claims bonus.

GRAMMAR

'If language is not correct, then what is said is not what is meant; if what is said is not what is meant, then what ought to be done remains undone.' So wrote Confucius some five hundred years before the birth of Christ, and his statement is as true today as it ever was. To be correct in one's use of language — and that means following the rules of grammar — makes it as certain as it ever can be that one's reader will get the intended message. Since the only reason for writing a letter is to tell your reader something, it follows that grammatical correctness is imperative. To write incorrectly will not only give a bad impression but, perhaps even more seriously, it may lead to confusion and misunderstanding.

Unfortunately for the average letter writer, language is a living entity and correct usage changes over the years. Furthermore, constructions which you may 'get away with' in daily conversation may not be grammatically acceptable in writing prose. The gap between what we 'get away with' in speech and what is correct in writing presents considerable difficulty to many people. The rules of English grammar are extremely complicated, but for the purposes of letter writing it is sufficient to be familiar with the basic structure of a correct sentence and the rules of proper punctuation. If you know those, and avoid trying to write long and complex sentences you should avoid many mistakes. Keep a dictionary beside you to check any spellings of which you are unsure, and be aware of the common pitfalls listed in this chapter.

There is only room to include the basic points of grammar here. Several more comprehensive books on the use of grammar are available.

The sentence

A sentence is defined as a group of words which make complete sense. In order to do this, it must contain two parts: the subject, a word or words about which the sentence will say something, and a predicate, a word or words about the subject. For example, in the sentence

 The boy stole an apple.

the first part, the boy, is the subject, and the second part, stole an apple, is the predicate.

Note the following guidelines when writing a sentence:

1 Avoid splitting your subject and predicate.
 Do not write:

   David, after fighting with John at the park, repented.

 Write:

   After fighting with John at the park, David repented.

2   Avoid splitting an infinitive (to run, to walk, to obey, etc.)
Do not write:
> Peter wanted to carefully and meticulously stick the stamps in his album.

Write:
> Peter wanted to stick the stamps in his album carefully and meticulously.

3   Keep the same subject.
Do not write:
> We were cold at the seaside because one felt the wind.

Write:
> We were cold at the seaside because we felt the wind.

4   Keep the same tense.
Do not write:
> Jane answered the telephone but nobody speaks.

Write:
> Jane answered the telephone but nobody spoke.

Some grammatical pitfalls

1   Collective nouns

Collective nouns are nouns which are singular in form but refer to a group of persons or things. One must be careful to use a singular or a plural verb depending on the purpose of the particular sentence.

> The committee was furious with the plans for a strike.

That is, the committee was acting as a group.

> The committee were arguing among themselves over the plans for a strike.

That is, the committee were obviously acting as individuals, not as a unit.

2   Pronouns

The most common error involving pronouns is in phrases using 'me' and 'I'. For example, 'between you and I' should be 'between you and me'.

3   Adjectives

Similar to the problem of the collective noun is the problem of 'distributive' adjectives and pronouns. These are: anybody, nobody, everybody, either, neither, each, every, none. They are all singular, and must be used with verbs and pronouns in the singular.

Do not write:
> Everybody who travels abroad must have their passports.

Write:
> Everybody who travels abroad must have his passport.

And, do not write:
> Each of the children were given balloons after the party.

Write:
> Each of the children was given a balloon after the party.

4   Verbs

Verbs are singular or plural depending on the singular or plural nature of their subject.

a) It is correct to write, either:

      Those dishes, left from Julie's party, have not been washed.

    Or, to write:

      That stack of dishes, left from Julie's party, has not been washed.

b) The use of 'and', is like the plus sign in mathematics and makes a plural total.

      John and Kathy were at the restaurant.

If we use any other words to join John and Kathy, this does not happen.

      John, as well as his girlfriend Kathy, was at the restaurant.

5 Adverbs

The most common mistake here is to use an adjective when an adverb is required.

    Do not write:

      She ate the biscuits very quick.

    Write:

      She ate the biscuits very quickly.

6 Prepositions

a) Avoid using the prepositional phrase 'due to' when 'because of' conveys the correct idea of causation.

    Do not write:

      The cricket match was stopped due to the rain.

    Write:

      The cricket match was stopped because of the rain.

b) Avoid using the verb 'following' when prepositions and prepositional phrases such as 'after', 'because of', 'as a result of', and 'in accordance with', are more accurate.

    Do not write:

      Following the heavy rains, the roads flooded.

    Write:

      Because of the heavy rains, the roads flooded.

      or

      After the heavy rains, the roads flooded.

7 Miscellaneous errors

a) Than

      John is cleverer than me.

This is incorrect because the complete sentence would be:

      John is cleverer than I am.

    Write:

      John is cleverer than I.

b) Less and fewer

'Fewer' should be used when the persons or objects referred to can be counted, use 'less' when what is referred to cannot be counted.

    Write:

      James ate no fewer than four biscuits at tea.

      James takes less sugar in his tea than I do.

The exception to this rule is in statements about time and distance.

      London is less than 32 kilometres from our country cottage, and it should take less than an hour to get there.

Punctuation

The most commonly used punctuation marks in English are:

full stop	.
colon	:
semicolon	;
comma	,
parentheses	()
question mark	?
exclamation mark	!
quotation marks	' '
apostrophe	'

1 Full stop

Every declarative sentence must end with a full stop.

2 Colon

The colon signals that an explanation or more information follows.

a) It is used to introduce a series.

> The child wanted three things for Christmas: a large stuffed animal, some coloured paper, and a small bicycle.

b) It is used to introduce a quotation.

> My mother's favourite saying is from Mark Twain: 'Work consists of whatever a body is obliged to do . . . Play consists of whatever a body is not obliged to do.'

c) It is used to separate two clauses of equal weight.

> Paul said it was time for supper: I said we had just finished lunch.

3 Semicolon

This functions mainly in a long sentence to separate clauses where a pause between a comma and a full stop is needed.

4 Comma

The comma is the most frequently used punctuation mark.

a) It is used to separate items in a list of three or more words.

b) It is used to separate phrases which depend on the same word.

> I have travelled in Canada in a canoe, in Egypt on a camel, and in England on a train.

c) It is used in a long sentence where a natural pause occurs.

5 Parentheses (sometimes known as brackets)

These are used in pairs when the writer has an interruption or aside not necessarily relevant to the main idea of the sentence.

6 Question mark

This is used at the end of a sentence which is a direct question.

> Is there any milk on the doorstep?

Do not use for an indirect question.

> Mother asked if there was any milk on the doorstep.

7 Exclamation mark

This mark is used at the end of a sentence when a strong feeling is present. A single exclamation is enough.

8 Quotation marks

These are used in pairs to enclose direct quotations.

> He asked, 'Where is my umbrella?'

Full stops and commas go inside the quotation marks when they directly relate to the matter quoted.

> Did he ask, 'Where is my umbrella'?

Do not use quotation marks to enclose slang, technical words in common use, or common phrases.

9 Apostrophe

The apostrophe is used as a mark of omission as in won't, can't or it's. It is also used to show possession, either singular or plural.

> This is Mary's hat. (singular)
> Where are the boy's clothes? (singular)
> Where are the boys' clothes? (plural; more than one boy)

Capital letters

Use an initial capital letter:

1 to begin a new sentence
2 to mark a proper noun or adjective (England, Englishman)
3 to write the days of the week and the months
4 to begin a full quotation
5 to write the names of companies, books, films, newspapers
6 to name specific courses (English Language 'O' Level)

Do not use the capital letter for general classes or names.

> Every American wants to be president.

Do not use for the seasons of the year.

Spelling

1 When you are unsure of a spelling, look up the word in a dictionary.
2 A simple jingle to remember when spelling words with 'ie' or 'ei' is:

> I before E, when sounded as E,
> Except after C
> Or when sounded as A
> As in neighbour or weigh.

3 Prefix

A prefix is one or more letters or syllables added to the beginning of a root word. When a prefix is added, the spelling of the root word remains unchanged.

> **dis appear** becomes **disappear**
> **over worked** becomes **overworked**

4 Suffix

A suffix is one or more letters or syllables added to the ending of a root word. Two rules to remember when adding suffixes are:

a) A silent 'e' is normally dropped before adding the suffix.

> **bore** becomes **boring**
> **change** becomes **changing**

b) Add a 'k' to words ending in 'c'.

> **picnic** becomes **picnicking**
> **panic** becomes **panicking**

Commonly misspelled words

accept (to receive)
affect (to influence)
all ready (entirely prepared)
allusion (reference)
elusion (escape)
baring (uncovering)
capital (city or letter)
complement (that which completes)

dependent (when used as an adjective)

dyeing (colouring)
formally (in a formal way)
forth (forward)
miner (mine worker)
personal (private)
principal (most important)

stationary (immobile)
weather (atmospheric conditions)

except (omit, excluding)
effect (result)
already (previously)
illusion (false impression)

bearing (carrying, withstanding)
capitol (building)
compliment (praise)

dependant (when used as a noun)

dying (near death)
formerly (at an earlier time)
fourth (4th)
minor (lesser or smaller)
personnel (staff)
principle (standard of conduct or fundamental truth)

stationery (writing supplies)
whether (conjunction)

Commonly misused words

alternatively means in a way which offers choice
appraise means to form a value judgment
imply means to suggest: a writer or speaker implies something
learn means to gain knowledge
disinterested means unbiased

i.e. (id est) means that is, and introduces a definition

alternately means by turns

apprise means to inform

infer means to conclude: a listener infers from what the speaker says
teach means to impart knowledge
uninterested means not interested

e.g. (exempli gratia) means for example

USEFUL ADDRESSES

Appointments

Equal Opportunities Commission
Overseas House
Quay Street
Manchester
M3 3HN

Advice and assistance for people who have lost or been refused jobs on grounds of their sex.

Commission for Racial Equality
Elliot House
10-12 Allington Street
London
SW1E 5EH

Advice and assistance for people who have lost or been refused jobs on racial grounds.

For other employment advice, training courses, etc. go to your local Job Centre.

Business

The Registrar of Companies
Companies Registration Office
Crown Way
Maindy
Cardiff
CF4 3UZ

For information on limited liability companies in England and Wales — such as whether they have gone into liquidation. For registering new companies in Scotland.

H.M. Customs and Excise — local VAT offices listed in local telephone directories.

British Standards Institution
2 Park Street
London
W1Y 2BS

Sets technical standards for the manufacture of industrial and consumer goods.

Retail Trading Standards Association
360/366 Oxford Street
London
W1N 0BT

Association of retailers and manufacturers to maintain high standards. Deals with complaints against members.

Association of Manufacturers of
Domestic Electrical Appliances
593 Hitchin Road
Stopslay
Luton
Beds
LU2 7UN

Members abide by a Code of Practice and the Association will help in disputes which a consumer cannot solve directly with the company concerned.

There are many more trade associations for individual areas of manufacture or service. They offer a variety of services to their members and to members of the general public. To find out whether there is an association that can help you, ask in your local library or Citizens' Advice Bureau.

Landlord and tenant

Commission for Racial Equality — see above, will also advise on cases of discrimination in housing.
Rent Officer — at the local council offices, deals with rent rebates.
Rent Tribunal or Rent Assessment — in the local telephone directory, will deal with cases of unfair rent; seek advice from your CAB first.

Money

Building Societies Association
14 Park Street
London
W1Y 4AL

Free general information on mortgages and investment in building societies.

British Insurance Association
Aldermary House
Queen Street
London
EC4 4JD

Free leaflets explaining about insurance (not life assurance), and will answer individual queries. Also investigates complaints against members.

Life Offices Association
Address as for BIA

As for BIA but concerned solely with life assurance.

Finance Houses Association,
14 Queen Anne's Gate
London
SW1H 9AG

General information about instalment credit, and will help with complaints about members.

Consumer Credit Division
Office of Fair Trading
Field House
15-25 Brean's Buildings
London
EC4A 1PR

Publishes leaflets on your rights in relation to credit, which can also be obtained from your CAB or local Trading Standards Department.

County Courts
Address in local telephone book.

Deal with civil claims, up to certain financial limits, for bad debts. A Free explanatory booklet can be obtained from court office.